ms. aligned
2

Detail of illustration by Súa Agapé

ms. aligned
2

Connie Pan

Pat Matsueda

Rebecca Thomas

El León Literary Arts
Berkeley

Published 2017 by
El León Literary Arts of Berkeley, California
elleonliteraryarts.org

ISBN 978-0-9891277-5-2
Printed in the United States of America

Designed by Peak Services
peakserviceshawaii.com

Cover illustration © Súa Agapé
suagape.com

Contents

Foreword

In Meditation XVII of his *Devotions upon Emergent Occasions,* John Donne wrote, "No man is an iland, intire of it selfe." He makes the case that each person is more whole through connection to others, and also that each of us is part of a greater whole. If we are to understand and experience this wholeness, this connection—to know it on a visceral level—we must first feel it, and what better way than through the compassion-inducing medium of literature? In this second volume of *Ms. Aligned,* the editors and authors continue a kind of conversation in literature regarding the many facets of men's lives as portrayed through women writers.

Of course, humanity is not divided simply between men and women, as in the purely masculine and the purely feminine. Instead, we exist on a spectrum, and, regardless of a physically defined gender or number of X chromosomes, we all share essentially the same hormones—androgens and estrogens, for example—in varying combinations. And those combinations express themselves in myriad ways.

We know this, and yet, whether out of convenience or culture or the mind's tendency to categorize, we often speak in binary terms of men or women. In fact, our artwork, media, icons, and legends often depict hypersexualized versions that become archetypal, even mythological. Unfortunately, those exaggerated portrayals create two potential problems. One is the risk that those who identify as male or female will feel a sense of inadequacy in comparison to the archetypes. The other is the risk of judging others based on preconceived notions and expectations for their appearance, behavior, capabilities, and character traits. As noted author and physician Dean Ornish writes, "Names and beliefs and preconceptions can bring a sense of order to the world, but often at the expense of being able to experience life fully."

Luckily for us, the authors in this collection, as well as editors Connie

Pan, Pat Matsueda, and Rebecca Thomas, have instead portrayed more nuanced representations of the masculine experience that begins with the archetypal and mythological, but troubles it, complicates it, causes us to challenge our own fundamental beliefs against a more complex and realistic array of expression. The challenge is not in being able to portray what is especially or particularly male. The challenge lies in portraying fully realized males, including those aspects of personality somehow deemed "feminine," even though those traits and behaviors are certainly not exclusive to women. It's human nature to see archetypes first, and takes the skill and intent of an attentive writer to write the exceptions, the quirks, the subtleties of behavior that transform a male character from being "a man" to being a multifaceted and unique individual.

Perhaps more importantly, these poems, stories, and personal narratives come to us from two perspectives. One, through the lens of female-identified writers who have spent much of their lives in close observation of the world around them. And two, through the lens of people who identify as female paying close attention to their interactions with men. Getting back to the words of John Donne, that no man is an island, these writings push us beyond superficial notions of masculinity, and even past the age-old conversation of trying to define what is male. Instead, they show us—through situation and story, through contact and conversation, through the very act of living among others—what it is to experience and be affected by various males we encounter. The stories grapple with fear and hope, inequity and injustice, but ultimately leave us with a richer, and, yes, more compassionate take on the world around us. Memorable stories that lay before us a feast of benevolence and care.

Jill McCabe Johnson, Ph.D.

Preface

During my time on Oʻahu, Pat Matsueda and I started a writing workshop. Every three weeks, four writers met at local eateries to share food and several pages of work. At La Tour Café, Pat, over espresso and tea, asked me to helm the next installment of *Ms. Aligned,* her brainchild, a labor of love. I didn't have to think; I said yes.

On a panel discussion with Connie Pan about diaspora, place, and identity, I read from a short story about a Mexican-American teenage boy. During the Q&A session, an audience member asked why I chose to write from his perspective. "What right do I, a white girl, have in writing about a Mexican-American teenage guy?" I asked. I understood her subtext, and she nodded. Although I think the woman's intention behind the question had more to do with culture and race than gender, it's something that has haunted me for years. I often wonder if the question would have been posed to a male author. While the concept of race might, gender rarely is.

When Connie discussed the first *Ms. Aligned* anthology years later, I instantly thought of that panel. What right do we have, the woman asked. It's a question I know Connie has considered as she writes stories from male points of view, and it's a question that I find gets addressed to women more than men—how can we possibly write from such different experiences?

And yet, this is what writers do. We gain empathy, we gain understanding, by considering others, by attempting to imagine someone else's viewpoint. As women writers, we have to fight to get our voices and our perspectives heard. This seems especially true when we are writing about experiences other than our own.

The *Ms. Aligned* series creates a space for women to explore the male worldview, to insert our voices and our perception of the world through the male lens. I was enamored with the first anthology when it came out. So, when Connie asked me to be a part of the *Ms. Aligned 2* team, I jumped at the opportunity.

Rebecca and I group-text religiously with two women from our writing program. Recently, one expressed her frustration with the lack of female mentors she had. Yes, we sympathized. There are undeniably gaps, and this needs to change; we are working, tirelessly, to change this. Navigating rooms where no one looks like me is lonely, but—sometimes with the right person in the right moment with love, luck, and sun—from loneliness sprouts great things, like sisterhood, like *Ms. Aligned*, like change.

While reading, something Rachel Carson wrote touched me: "No writer can stand still. He continues to create or he perishes. Each task completed carries its own obligation to go on to something new." Despite the antiquated reference to he and only he, I printed it, sealed it in an envelope, and mailed it across the Pacific to Pat because it resonated not only with *Ms. Aligned*'s mission but with our personal philosophies. As soon as the first *Ms. Aligned* entered the world, Pat began dreaming of the next.

Between the three of us, we are partners, mothers, sisters, and full-time workers in the publishing, corporate, and academic worlds; we are entrepreneurs, freelancers, and volunteers. In every role, at our very essence, lives the writer. Artists who attempt to render a world beautifully, and a beautiful world is not one that stamps out the voice of women. A beautiful world, with Chimamanda Ngozi Adichie's "The Danger of a Single Story" in mind, is not one where "a single story" represents all stories. A beautiful world is not one where someone can't find herself in its history, its present, or imagine herself in its future. A beautiful world is inclusive, expansive, respectful, and in the service of others. We saw an absence in the canon, and the *Ms. Aligned* series creates a space to begin the conversation.

Connie Pan and Rebecca Thomas

Introduction

Our lawnmower lives in the garage beneath a drop-down table on which my husband has balanced a whiteboard. A series of trigonometric calculations snake across the surface in blue and green Expo pen. As I maneuver the mower past numbers and angles, beyond the shelving unit filled with neatly organized chisels and hammers, clamps and blades, I notice a burl of wood.

My husband is an engineer, so it is generally accepted that I am the artist in our relationship. When not teaching, I slip through my days in soft-pants and sweatshirts, sipping coffee and murmuring to myself. I hole up in the attic beside a window and write. When my husband's not working, he's often found in the garage, a respirator covering his face, planing timber. He owned, for close to a decade, a 48-foot wooden sailboat. Later, he learned to timber-frame a house. These days our small garage serves as a downsized workshop from which emerges useful items: a pair of sawhorses, shelves for the basement, a frame for a couch.

But this burl is something new. I remember, vaguely, his taking a trip to a local wood dealer to buy black walnut. The older gentleman said that for $30 he'd throw in something extra: three chunks of dull, gray wood. For some reason, my husband agreed. The wood had once composed a whole cross-section of a tree, but it hadn't been dried properly, so it split. Since then, each piece had cracked further, been scratched, aged to a color resembling rat fur.

But my husband saw something in these throwaway pieces, and he took his hand to them. Now, somehow, the burl is whole, a single round, planed and smooth. In the dusty light, the surface glows amber, and the rings within the wood give it a sense of depth, as if I am peering into a canyon.

The rest of the day, I see our home in a new way. The oak bookshelf my husband built, the sides sanded in an undulating pattern so that running our hands along the surface would feel like riding waves in the Pacific. My desk, constructed of purpleheart and mahogany, with a koa wood live edge so that my hands would always be resting on native Hawaiian wood. Elsewhere in the house, I find a book on mission-style furniture designs and my space heater covered in wood dust. (What was he doing with *that* this summer?) It's not that I feel my husband has been leading some other life without me; rather, it's that as much as I see him, listen to him, share with him, he contains depths that are unknowable to me. Why did he give such attention to this burl? Why did it matter to him to draw out its beauty like this? What was it like for him to make this segmented thing whole again?

In the first *Ms. Aligned* anthology, I noticed a theme of beloved-ness. In my afterword, I asked: "How could any of us have planned to love these men—real men, imagined men—so much that we would memorialize them on paper? How could we have ever foreseen understanding them as we do, even if that understanding comes from writing them?"

In this second anthology, there arises, for me, a twinned notion: that it is impossible to know every depth of another; and yet, from the desire to bridge that unknowing springs tenderness, growth, and beauty. We can never completely know someone, and yet we must keep trying to.

In *Ms. Aligned 2*, this theme appears in delightful, unexpected ways. A Sasquatch leaves his "prints in mud" in hopes that a woman he once saw will believe in him; a friend of a fisherman's son listens to stories that reveal and conceal in equal measure; an apprentice shaman spends years listening to nothing in the belief he will one day connect with spirits. In Sion Dayson's story "Metal Man," the narrator says to a woman with whom he's falling in love that he thinks "maybe we're just too different. It's not going to work out." But then the narrative turns. The story is not about their difference, nor even really about the potential for their relationship, but about something else—artistic endeavor and discovering the depths of one's self. In each of these stories and poems, it's the reaching out, the trying to understand, that creates the emotional center of the piece.

Adele Ne Jame moves this question of reaching, of knowing and not-knowing, to a national level in her poem "A Deadly Embrace." She writes:

You may love Lebanon,

but it doesn't love you back
my father might have said after
it showed us Death on this mountain.

In Ne Jame's poetry, we feel the tension of love and threat, of motherland and father's warning. The speaker draws close—draws us close—to understanding this place, its complex history, even as understanding the terror and violence that the poem references is near impossible. In the end, exile, vacancy, a rusted iron drum that "collects pure water for no one" fills the scene. This is the aftermath: loss, grief, emptiness.

Like Ne Jame's poems, the work in this anthology uses juxtaposition—of closeness and distance, of knowing and not knowing, of terror and hope—to offer insight. The writers elide simple answers and instead give us images, jarring and impossible in their truth, so that we might experience the worlds they illustrate. As Amy Holwerda, the author of "Gardenia," notes in her artist's statement: "We all have these sensory memories imprinted on our subconscious and know how the sudden smell of clove cigarettes or musty book pages can jolt us into sudden awareness, even when the memory cannot be immediately identified." So, too, with the work in this anthology, which jolts its reader into an awareness of these characters, their worlds, their sheer sensory reality.

The writers plumb not only the depths of their characters but also, it seems, their own depths. Two pieces in particular—Angela Nishimoto's "Sex Education: A Tragicomedy of Seven Years" and Connie Pan's "Because We Need Evidence"—hold up mirrors to the experience of being a woman. And here is another way that this second anthology from *Ms. Aligned* gives its readers fresh material: as much as these women writers are writing men, they are also women writing women and the female experience. In this act, they make a segmentation—of gender, experience, place, age—whole again.

In Cassandra Lane's nonfiction piece "Day of Venus," a young son looks from his mother to a marble sculpture of Venus, "perhaps wondering what his brown-skinned, dreadlocked mommy could possibly have in common with the pale, marbleized goddess." A tension lies in this bind: to deny a similarity to Venus is to deny the narrator's own beauty, her own Aphroditic needs. But to accept Venus as a mirror is to negate her own history, her brown skin, her dreadlocked hair. Instead, the narrator must find something that reflects her whole self, that can help lead her and her son into a more integrated future. She must find her own way forward.

So, too, these authors. To read *Ms Aligned 2* is to witness women writers writing forward—out of old tropes, expected ways of being, and into something fresh, memorable, filled with discovery.

A few days after I've drafted this introduction, my husband and I are in the garage. He's building a base for the burl so that it can serve as a side table. He's made wooden triangles, hollow on the inside and oddly delicate, and he's stacking them by size so that they get progressively smaller as they reach upwards.

"If I had sanded this burl forever," he says, motioning to the heavy piece still on the ground, "there would have been nothing left. Just wood dust. Instead, I had to decide at some point that what was there was beautiful. It was perfect just the way it was."

He takes a cloth and wipes the burl's surfaces. Indeed, it has its unique traits: a dark-colored seam where he tinted the epoxy with coffee grounds, a series of grooves he filled with Elmer's glue and sanded smooth, an edge that remains ash-colored because he didn't want to plane away the bumpy surface. But these "imperfections" give the table character, make it seem as if it lived many lives before it came to us.

"You know," he continues, "I think it's about accepting someone or something as they are. All the cracks, the scratches, the stuff from the past. For me, that's what this burl is really about."

I think of this introduction, the stories and poems in *Ms. Aligned 2*. How writing can deepen understanding even if it can never uncover every depth. Acceptance, then, is not just about taking someone as they are, imperfections and all. It's also about the acceptance of mystery, of never quite bridging a divine divide between what I know—of another, of myself—and what is still available to discover. What a delightful idea, I think to myself. How wonderful to recognize in these works both the connections made and the human mystery that remains.

My husband, still focused on the table, heaves the thick burl into the air and then carefully sets it on the top triangle. I gasp, afraid the whole thing will tumble before he has a chance to secure it. But the burl remains somehow, perfectly balanced on this precarious cairn. "How did you do that?"

"I don't know," he admits. "But do you like it?"

"Yes," I nod. "I love it."

"Well then," he says, "that's enough for me."

Kristiana Kahakauwila

Cassandra Lane

Day of Venus

In one of our many mommy-and-me outings, my son and I are partici-
pating in a Getty Museum tour called "Move," a concept of engaging our
bodies, not just our eyes and heads, to explore artwork in an interactive
"physical conversation." Along with the rest of the people in our group, we
twist our limbs and faces to mimic statues, furniture, and images in paint-
ings, setting off riffs of giggles as we behold each other's awkwardness.

Our docent, Andrew, eggs all of us on. "Wonderful! Beautiful!"

"Now, tell us," he says, turning to one woman, "why do you have your
arm up over your head in that way? And what is it that your elbow is
doing?"

"I'm trying to capture the elegance of the bed's head frame, which is
curvy and tall, but also has sharp edges around it, which I guess is why
my elbows are sticking out like this," the woman answers. The group
chuckles.

"Lovely," Andrew says, and the rest of us rub our hands together for a
soft applause. Our palms produce a swishing sound. Andrew leads us into
another gallery, populated with white, life-size marble statues of Roman
gods and goddesses—those symbols of supposed purity, beauty, and sen-
suality. Solomon, who has just turned seven ("The age of enlightenment,"
I always tell him), tugs on my arm and asks, in his library-voice: "Why are
so many of them naked?" He aims his forefinger at the figurines. His side
is pinned to mine, a magnet.

"Because it's art," I respond, peeling away from him. "It's not really
about being naked, sweetie."

Andrew instructs us to walk around the room, quietly studying the
various statues and busts.

"Find the one that speaks to you," he says, taking time to search out each of our eyes. Andrew's eyes twinkle with mischief as he stands, his beanstalk body bent like a reed in the wind—long, lean, limber. His clothing follows the singular fluid instrument that is his body. A solid black yarmulke is glued to the back of his small head, an anchor that seems to pull his chin upward, where it hovers like the tip of a crane over the rest of his body.

"In about five minutes, we will all return to the center of the room," Andrew says, raising his right hand. His slender fingers freeze against the air like the limbs of a praying mantis.

"One by one, each of us will strike a pose, mimicking the artwork that we have chosen, and those of us looking on will have to guess the statue in question," he says, his words popping with excitement.

Giddy, Solomon follows me to a corner of the gallery curating the Judgment of Paris. We see the young Paris looking at Minerva, the helmeted goddess of war and strategy, as Venus and Juno vie for Paris's attention, trying to sway the judge, with their seductive beauty, to choose one of them as the fairest.

It is this Roman myth that lay at the foundation of the fairy tales I read openly as a girl ("Mirror, Mirror, on the Wall, who's the fairest of them of all?"). It was this myth that showed up again and again in my mother's Harlequin and Silhouette romance novels that I used to sneak and devour. And it was this myth that inserted itself in the battle between my sister Dena and me when we were teenagers. "Don't you wish your girlfriend was as beautiful as this?" she hissed one night, thrusting "this," her perfectly made-up, diamond-shaped face—an enviable contrast to my wide one—in my boyfriend's face, foreshadowing a modern-day pop song, "Don't You Wish Your Girlfriend Was Hot Like Me?", that I would find myself triumphantly singing and winding my hips to while in the throes of an affair, except his "girlfriend" was his wife. And I was more than his hot girlfriend; I, too, was somebody else's spouse. Vince's wife.

But that was a lifetime ago.

I have given birth to new life since then. And in that birthing, have hoped that I, too, have been reborn. I met Michael at the end of my affair, before Vince and I had drawn up our divorce papers. Michael, too, was in the middle of a divorce, with full custody of two shell-shocked pubescent sons and a penchant for too much wine, a no-no since he was a recovering cocaine addict, with the same number of years clean as the age of his youngest child, Niko, who was 11 at the time.

Given the 80s, the time period in which Michael was an addict, and his economic and geographical status—struggling in South LA—the powder in question was not, most likely, pure cocaine. Not that I knew much about the crack epidemic. I had grown up fairly gated from all that in small-town Louisiana, and had believed I was dying the one time I tried to smoke a cigarette. Besides a few drunken nights and nasty hangovers in college, I had no inkling what a life of substance abuse was like.

So we danced our way into each other's lives, Michael and I. Our starting point of the maze was a nightclub filled with cushiony benches draped in red and gold fabric, surrounded by the bass-boom of neo-soul, statues of the Buddha, and mostly early- to mid-30-year-olds, who schmoozed and danced until 2 a.m. The club, Little Temple, was just blocks away from the one-bedroom Silverlake-adjacent apartment Michael shared with his sons. The wine or the music or both aided us in believing what we wanted to believe: that we could save each other and ourselves because, after all, we had so much in common and so much passion between us and were so in love.

A year and a half later, we had a baby and named him Solomon, subconsciously calling upon this poor child's head a legacy of romantic lust and betrayal. Of multiple wives and concubines and mournful poetics: "I have seen all the things that are done under the sun; all of them are meaningless, a chasing after the wind," King Solomon wrote. "Vanity of vanities. All is vanity!"

I had grown up in the church, and had always loved the name Solomon and the story of the king who saved a baby's life by threatening to cut him in half to draw out the truth from the real mother and the ruthlessness from the false one. Michael followed my lead in the naming; he had always loved the name for its sound of strength. I should have known better—about the power of names, about the crossed wires of desire and hope. Still, with my breasts full of un-pumped milk, Michael and I drove to Vegas one August weekend, leaving our one-year-old baby behind in Los Angeles with Michael's mother and Niko. I texted a slew of friends and family: "We're getting hitched in LV! Keeping it light, fun and sweet!" My dress was made of soft cotton: creamy yellow with eyelets and a halter tie. Springy and pretty and sexy and, well, sweet.

I read the stream of text responses aloud to Michael as he drove. We laughed together, feeling the highway air on our skin as we headed to our second marriages. We were grown. We had seen ugly and we had been ugly, and we were not afraid.

After turning from my Christian upbringing in junior high school, I spent whole days that evolved into years pursuing one thread after another to find myself, to understand others. Astrology and numerology. Name analyses and personality profile systems. Chakra and pendulum readings.

My friends sat under my investigations for the readings of astrological charts. A Taurus sun with Libra rising, I told them I was ruled by Venus, and this vision permeated my approach to chart readings. Two people I had a sudden flash to put together ended up getting married, which sent swarms of folks flocking to me like moths, clutching their birth details and desires. I obsessed over the symbols, dissecting and synthesizing angles and degrees and images, uncovering problems and predicting destinies.

"You take this symbolism thing way too far," my friend Nelson, a poet, said fourteen years ago in New Orleans. "Everything is not a sign, Sand."

"Shut up," I said, laughing. "Yes—it is."

Yet in all my searching and acquiring, I became more lost than ever. Doomed to remain the nearsighted girl roaming frantically down a maze of hallways at her new high school, too vain to don her eyeglasses, too proud, too scared, to ask for help. Instead, she pretends she is just headed to her locker whenever someone passes, or going to the girl's bathroom there, just beyond their shoulders. Each door she tries is locked or ends up being the janitor's broom closet, and so she turns again, choking back panic.

At the Getty, Solomon and I are dwarfed by massive cathedral ceilings. We are like ants, milling under ceilings and lights and in between the raised statues in awe. Solomon cranes his neck, looking at me looking at the larger-than-life depictions of my old obsessions, frozen in gray-white marble. I think of the ancient Israelites and their worship of inanimate gods, and acknowledge, with a swift flood of compassion, our need as humans to see our desires and faith materialized.

I gaze at Venus's eyeballs—white and eerie. "Aphrodite," I whisper, calling out her Greek name. I didn't learn of the likes of African goddesses such as Seshet, Oya or Oshun until I was an adult living in New Orleans, surrounded by blackness and beauty; mystery and history.

"You are Aphrodite, my dear," a friend who studies and teaches mythology and writes poetry and fiction, once told me from the house she and her husband shared in the hills of Playa del Rey, overlooking the Pacific Ocean through a floor-to-ceiling window. I had confided in her that Vince was leaving our marriage after I revealed to him that I was having an affair.

"Vince is a great guy—we love him—but he was not feeding your sensual side," Kate said. 'He's Hephaestus—all work, work, work. Well, that's not what Aphrodite needs."

I study Venus's body—the smooth curve of breasts, her long fleshy waist, dimpling in at the navel, the wide expanse of hips flowing into ample thighs. It was my own body, to some degree, though, unlike the proud look on her face, I do not brazenly embrace the fleshier parts of me. I cringe at the curves in my abdomen, at the recent thickening of thighs, at the already generous hips expanded by the shifting of pelvic bones during childbirth. Though I work out relentlessly, I feel and see the changes in my 40-plus-year-old body—the heaviness, the fleshiness that appeared like unwanted magic. My knee and foot bones sometimes crack with pain that I ignore during workouts.

In hot yoga, whenever the teacher urges us to hold the eagle pose, I try hard to acquiesce. "This is the pose that melts away all that cellulite," she likes to say, and my heart skips a little.

"Squeeze, squeeze, squeeze," she insists. "Squeeze your thighs together as though you are wringing every drop of water out of a towel."

And I squeeze, trying not to notice the sweat pouring from my scalp, my eyelashes, the dizziness that threatens to overcome me.

"Point your toes in the direction you want your leg to go and your body will follow," the teacher is fond of saying. As I teeter-totter, one arm hooked under the other, trying to keep my hands together under my chin in the pose that stretches the tight muscles in my upper back, shoulders and triceps, while also trying to wring my thighs like a towel, my balance always fails me, and I topple over ungracefully.

Venus, on the other hand, makes bending with one leg propped against the other look effortless.

"Is she the one you're going to pick, Mommy?" Sol asks. He looks from me to Venus, perhaps wondering what his brown-skinned, dreadlocked mommy could possibly have in common with the pale, marbleized goddess.

"I don't know yet, son," I say, stepping backwards slowly, still in view of Venus's white sockets.

Emily A. Benton

Sasquatch in Love

How he pines among the needles and firs
for the nudist he once saw bathing by
the waterfall. For the moment she turned,
when a finch left the brush and her tame eye
almost caught his. How he wanted to reach
out and touch her, tuck her lilywhite hair
behind her ear, feed her blackberries he'd
plucked, gift her honeysuckle from his beard.
But she is gone, and she did not see him.
For he is left to roam with plants alone.
Thus he sulks in the vastness of his den
and remote woods. *If only she could know
I exist,* he thinks and paces and leaves
prints in mud: small signs should she believe.

Mary Archer

Death of Blossom Girl

Millions of miles away, a stranger goes on some strange wind blowing stranger still. How would a girl of one and twenty know how strange things would go?

One fine day, the air did catch some chilly breeze that pricked her skin. Oh, the chill that chilled her then. Some way, somehow, in the knowing place she knew, this wind did touch her true.

The odious were close. "Yet don't fly," the wind did say. "Stay."

"But wind," the girl said. "The breeze. Your breeze and all the trees say, 'Leave.'"

"Girl, believe" was all the wind did say. What else could blossom girl do?

Her traveler cape hid her young breasts, but these some men did see. They bit where lovers suckled and babies drew. They bit for blood, these careless men, these bloodless men. Fresh, her bosom leaked red.

She grew thin, her heart bore ill, she was nothing but a shadow on the wind. She was little caring then. Herself she was tearing then. She cried hate and bled where she was bitten and her loins ached. But still, what could blossom girl do? She bit her tongue so hard, blood she drew.

They raped her every fourth Thursday. They did what foul men do. Forsaken, blossom girl cried, "Wind! Bear witness. See all these men take!" But there was nothing—nothing but the chill to trace the wind.

She sobbed and hurt where the hurting was fresh. Ants laced her clothes where the men had stained her deep. Under a shroud of tree, she wept and the tears blamed the hollow where she slept.

Who was she, this pitiable mound of flesh? Who was she, this meal for men? Fire grew from her heart, and fire grew the hate that birthed in her.

"*Z*ounds," the hills did cry. "Your bleeding, blossom girl, is waking the slumbering dead to your tears. Dry yourself, girl, no more is needed from you hence. Bind yourself. Bind your bleeding, you wretch."

But would she listen? The girl—plaintive, loud, and lasting—caused the roasting old bones to turn. The hills seethed, "You foul my shelter with sweating tears, girl. Relieve me or be killed."

Now the girl, unblossomed, said, "You deny me everything. You deny me dirt. You deny me rest." The fire in her flaring, the girl stood. "Make me hear you or make me dead."

"You pitiful thing. We lie, the winds and hills. Don't bargain for our truths."

And the girl, quieting, sighed, "So be it."

So the wind and hills killed the blossom girl, and no more were Thursdays red.

Connie Pan

Because We Need Evidence, Send His Emails Somewhere You Don't Have to See Them

label: don't-open

STILL——I find your hair everywhere. It won't let me forget you, that	1:33 am
(no subject)——I wonder about you. I hope one day I can stop	Feb 2
My letter——What I really meant to write, "I promise, if you let me, I'll keep up." I	1/7/16
Rereading your letters——I'm sorry I didn't listen. Please	12/29/15
I'll be in your state——I know you said that you don't want to see me, but	12/28/15
Thanksgiving——I heard you're in town. It kills me that I'm no longer a pri	11/23/15
Regrets——I want to call you every second of every day. Sometime	11/16/15
Happy Birthday!!!!——You're so amazing. I hope you received my gift. Have a ve	11/11/15
Unreasonable——I have always been honest with you. Your pettiness and pride	11/3/15
(no subject)——You sure are doing a great job of avoiding me. I hate your silen	11/1/15
One misstep——Look, I don't want your forgiveness. I just want	10/29/15
Lies——I saw your friends today. They seem to think——with your help——that I ki	10/28/15

Hi there——Let me show you how much I can love you. Nothin   10/27/15
Sorry——I don't know if or when my emails will stop. Maybe once I feel I ha   10/26/15
I'm sorry——I couldn't be the Pacific of love that you are. I can now. W   10/25/15
Earthquake——I saw the news. Please call, write, anything, so I kno   10/24/15
lyrics——I keep hearing this song, "I didn't know what I was doing until   10/23/15
(no subject)——Every time my phone rings I hope it's you. Is it silly   10/22/15
Curve——Don't seal me out of your life. That   10/22/15
I Know You Don't Want to Talk to Me——Is there anything I can do or say? My   10/22/15
About that night——As much as I wish Saturday didn't happen, I'm glad it did be   10/20/15
Extreme——You probably won't respond to this, but it'd be nice if   10/19/15
(no subject)——You were right. Now isn't the time. Sorry I   10/18/15
SHOCKED——I wish I could erase tonight. Don't let that be your last imp   10/18/15

Sion Dayson

Metal Man

Tonight's the first time Emily's asked me up to her place. We just had dinner, but now I'm excited the plan might include dessert. She has the perfect body. Since I first saw her, I've wondered what it would feel like pressed next to mine.

"Is that what I think it is?" I say, pointing towards a sculpture sitting on a side table.

"It's a fertility symbol," she says. "In the Kivasa tribe, they carve a new statue before each hunt. The man with the biggest kill is seen as the most virile and becomes the statue's keeper to bless the village with more children."

Emily takes a sip of wine while I try to take that in. "But yeah, it's a big phallus," she adds, laughing. "Does it make you uncomfortable?"

"Symbol of virility," I say. "I'm cool with that."

She laughs again, and I wipe my sweating palms on my jeans.

When I met her, Emily jangled and sparkled. Besides the instant jump you feel in the gut when you see a beautiful girl, I noticed how much noise she made as she moved. Tons of bracelets ran up both her arms. She wore several layers of scarves with tiny mirrors all over them; I saw myself in a million fractured pieces. She brought her car, an '87 Volkswagen Bug, into my garage for a routine oil change, but getting to know her has proved anything but routine.

"I'm still a little hungry. How about you?" she asks.

"I told you, soup never fills you up. You should have gone for the BBQ."

"No way. Mongolian barbecue isn't even Mongolian. It's a trend from Taiwan!"

I didn't even know Mongolian cuisine was a possibility before Emily suggested it.

"You sure you don't want anything?" she asks.

It seems like she does, so I say, "Why not."

"Go scrounge in the kitchen," she says. "Try the cupboard on the left—that's where I keep all my munchies."

I raise my eyebrows.

"I'd rather you just choose what you want. I keep springing new things on you." She brushes my knee with her hand. "You're sweet to humor me."

It's true, some of the things we've tried have been beyond me, but I like it. It's been interesting. That Chinggis vodka, for instance, just about knocked me out tonight.

I get up from the couch. Her kitchen is small and dark. I see a bowl of water on the floor and realize she must have a cat. It explains the odor. I haven't seen the cat yet.

I open one cabinet and there's nothing to eat, just things to eat on. Everything's mismatched. Plates of all different colors and sizes, some round, some square, all stacked high in one pile. There's an even more varied selection of beverage holders. A Rutgers anthropology thermos, an "I love Limpopo" mug, a shot glass with a leprechaun on it that looks more like a child with Down's syndrome. I feel like I'm spying.

I move to the next cupboard and open it up. There, taped up to the shelf, is a white piece of paper with the following words written in hurried cursive: "would you like to sleep here tonight?"

I read the sign again, and turn around, as if she might be behind me, then grin.

She's looking straight at me when I come back into the room, which also surprises me.

"Find anything good?" she asks.

"Yeah," I say.

"So?"

"You bet."

I'm not sure whether it's the vodka or the crude cock in the living room, but I have trouble getting it up at first. And that has never happened to me. Really.

"I don't know what's going on," I say.

"No big deal," she says. "Sometimes it's good to just slow down." If I weren't so relieved I might have felt offended that she didn't appear to care either way whether we did it or not. I could hardly believe this girl even let me get to this point; then once I'm there, nothing.

"Actually, I really did just want to sleep with you," she says, laying her head on my chest. "You make me feel...I don't know. Safe."

I swell at this, but the moment for that has passed. She's already dozing off, like it's the most normal thing in the world that I'm next to her. I am wired awake, aware of every sensation. Though I'm ready now, and practically high on her smell of pure girl clean, I feel lucky even to be holding her.

The guys are giving me a hard time today over my stubble and yesterday's clothes. I'm a clean freak—which makes no sense, as I'm basically dirty all day—and they can see that I haven't been home.

"So, Mike," they say, "how's the pretty professor?"

"She's not a professor. She's a PhD student."

"Same damn thing," Phil says. Of all of them, he's the most resentful. The others just think it's hilarious.

"But how was it?" Joe asks. "She's so smart, she know anything about fucking we don't?"

"Fuck off," I say and roll underneath the Ford that was brought in leaking brake fluid. I can see the problem right away, the hole from which the yellow liquid falls. It always puzzles me, why it is that people never seem to notice until too late that they've scraped the bottom, that something must be done.

As I work on the problem—replacing the master cylinder, sealing the reservoir with new washers—I think about all the things Emily does know. Things I didn't even know existed to know. I can tell her how to fix a transmission, when the fan belt needs replacing, the sound the motor mount makes when it starts coming loose. I can only imagine how thrilling that must be for her.

Phil comes and kicks my leg.

"Jesus," I say. "What's the matter with you?"

"I wouldn't get too close to that girl," Phil says. "You're just a passing fancy to a chick like that."

I sneer and roll back underneath the car. I hide there because I don't want him to see that I'd been thinking the same thing.

The next time we meet at a laundromat. "I've been in my pj's for the last 3 days," she said on the phone. She had a big paper due and was too stressed to go out. "I should do laundry."

I've started getting used to our unconventional dates—a simulated archaeological dig at a natural history museum, a random county fair—but I had to tease her about the idea of meeting at Suds and Duds.

"I've had dates that felt like chores before, but never a chore dressed up as a date," I said.

"Come on, you must have some boxers or socks or something," she said. "I want to see you."

I wanted to see her, too, and really, what else do I have to do?

When I arrive, she's already stuffing all of her clothes into one overworked machine. She hasn't bothered to change into street clothes. "I think better in my pajamas," she says as she retrieves a bra that's dropped to the floor and shoves it in.

She didn't need to change, as far as I'm concerned. She looks great. Her messy hair makes me imagine her coming straight from bed. I try not to get distracted.

I look around. The place is sketchy; I wonder when anything besides clothes was washed in here. Several machines have "out of order" signs scrawled on them.

"You don't separate colors and whites?" I say, as she shuts the door.

"No," she says, seeming to find my question amusing. "Why would I?"

I look around for a smaller machine—they're towards the back. I open door 11—my lucky number—and examine it. By the time I'm done with my inspection, Emily is already next to me.

"Wow, you're really thorough," she says. I've emptied the lint compartment, run a finger inside the machine for traces of dust, made sure there's no leftover sundries from the last person—a child's crayon, or some pocket change.

"You actually wear those?" she says. "I can't think of the last time I saw a guy in overalls."

"Well, yeah, they're useful. To hang tools and stuff. Lots of pockets."

"That's awesome," she says.

I'm a little embarrassed to have her looking over my shoulder. I wonder if she will mock my fabric softener. She doesn't.

When the business of loading the machines is over, we sit on a table used for folding clothes. We listen to the humming of the machines and make up stories about the few other people in the laundromat. She invents much more imaginative things than I do. She reads every detail of a person, things I wouldn't even notice. I say that none of them would guess we were on a date, when she asks what I think, though they probably know we're talking about them.

About halfway into the wash cycle, Emily's machine starts malfunctioning. Even from where we are, we can see the whole thing vibrating.

"Oh shit," she says and jumps up. She pounds on the door, which only increases the thumping noise. The entire window is filled with bubbles. It's impossible to even see any clothes through the foam.

"How much detergent did you put in there?" I ask, trying to stifle a laugh.

"I thought the box was almost empty so I dumped all the rest in. Hey," she says, placing her hand on the glass, "the clothes aren't even spinning around. I think something's wrong with this machine. Look, it's like it's stuck or something."

She opens the door and water pours out of the machine. She is the one soaked, but I am shocked. Those doors are usually locked solid.

"Oh my god," she says. "I'm so dumb."

"Here," I say, unbuttoning my shirt, "take this." The other people in the laundromat have cleared away from the quickly expanding puddle, but none of them say anything. They're watching like we're that afternoon's sitcom.

"Hold on," I say, and go to the back. I find a closet with a mop and bucket. I make quick work of the scene, while Emily stuffs her wet laundry back into her suitcase. She hasn't even bothered to take her wet shirt off—she has simply put mine on top.

"Well, that certainly woke me up," she says, laughing. "Alert for the next round." I tell her I can probably fix the machine if she wants.

"I should get back to my paper, anyway," she says. "At least I don't need to take a shower now. Multitasking." She lays her hand on my chest—I am now only in my undershirt—and gives me a long kiss. "And thanks," she says, looking around the newly mopped floor. "You're wonderful."

She turns and starts trying to lug her heavy suitcase out the door. I don't think about why she doesn't put her laundry in the dryer or what she will do with all those wet, soapy clothes. I am lightheaded. My heart thumps in time to the machine.

"Hey, let me," I say finally finding my words, taking the suitcase handle and rolling it toward the door. "I'll get my stuff later."

"Oh you," she says. "You're too good to me." We make our way to her apartment, just around the corner.

"Where should I put this?" I ask when we get in.

"That's fine," she says, waving her hand.

There's an awkward silence.

"Well, I won't keep you," I say.

"Oh, that's ok. Now that you're here…." She trails off. "I could take a break for a little longer."

I like what she has in mind. Her already ready for bed in her pj's, me already down to my undershirt.

This time, there's no trouble. I'm switched on high. We move with each other easily, fast and smooth as the spin cycle.

I'm cleaning my cell phone when she calls, like I had just wiped the plastic in order to see her name light up the screen, unstreaked and shining.

"Swing by at closing time?" she says, with no formalities, when I answer.

"Why don't we meet at McDuffy's at 8?" I say. "Give me a chance to clean up."

"I like it when you're dirty," she says.

I laugh. "Whatever you want." And it's true. I have come to the point where I will drop anything to be with this girl.

After I've hung up the phone Phil passes and remarks, "More errands?"

"Drink," I say. I should have never told him about the laundry.

Phil snorts. The thing about Phil is, he got burned a long time ago, but I'm thinking, who hasn't? His ex-wife had been a lawyer, never stopped cross-examining him. When Emily came in here that first time, all questions and energy, I think it must have reminded him somehow. There's no use in telling him that Emily's only curious, it's part of her charm.

I won't tell him anything more about her. I won't tell anyone, actually. It's becoming too personal to share. Would anyone understand that even if it had been a call to come fix her microwave or vacuum cat hair from her rug, I would have gone?

Whatever Emily wants, I am willing to do.

It's hot and stuffy at McDuffy's. Karaoke night, and someone's singing Loretta Lynn. I roll my eyes, thinking this would not be something Emily would like, but she's enjoying herself. She seems to feel at home wherever she is; it's something I wouldn't mind learning from her.

"So in our urban cultures class we have to choose a subculture in which to conduct our ethnographic research," Emily's saying, as she munches on potato chips.

"Umm-hmm," I say. Her version of bar talk cracks me up.

"I was thinking, why don't I use your garage as my subculture? Every workplace has its own culture, and I can imagine mechanics have their own codes and norms."

"Norms," I repeat.

"And it's especially interesting here, where there's good public transportation. The people who have cars, there's a certain status there. That must put you into contact with some interesting clientele."

"You could say that," I say, giving her a private grin.

Emily doesn't pick up on it, that she is the interesting clientele. She's on a roll. "What is that interaction like?" she's saying. "How is that space mediated? The interplay of server/customer, laborer and the public, the working class and the privileged? What do you think?"

I put my drink down. I'm not sure if I've chugged the beer down too fast, inhaled too much foam, but the bubbles are trapped in my chest.

"What are you asking me now?"

"Can I hang out at your garage? Take notes? Study the culture."

"The guys don't have much culture to speak of," I say, trying to make a joke of it.

"No, but you are your own culture. That's what I'm trying to say."

It's starting to be more than uncomfortable, the discomfort in my chest.

"You want to study me?" I say.

"Do a report. It's called an ethnography. I just want permission to enter your space. Act like I'm not there."

"That," I say, "would be impossible."

"Come on," she says. "I can blend in. Be a participant observer."

"This is your homework? Writing about being a mechanic?"

"Why not?"

By this point, the pain in my chest is really getting to me. I excuse myself to go to the bathroom. As I walk past the stage, I realize the woman singing is that girl Kathy I had gone out with a few times before I met Emily. Her caked on makeup is running and she sways like she's had one too many already.

In the bathroom, I stand at the sink for a few moments but nothing happens. I hear Kathy's warbling drift in: "A place to hide and cry a place to try and die..." Kathy, the kind of girl people think I should be with. I imagine Emily sitting out there nodding her head along to the song, filing away mental notes, drawing conclusions about who Kathy is because of the song she is singing.

I stare in the mirror. Is this what she's been thinking about the whole time? Those were her very words: laborer, server, working class.

I'm unable to dislodge the trapped air in my chest. I punch it, but the pressure there doesn't go away.

When I go back into the bar I make an excuse and get the hell out of there. The mopey soundtrack follows me out the door.

The guys know not to ask, but it's not lost on anyone that I've been spending more time out back this week, blowtorch in hand, mask over my face. I've made a large pile of things just lying around the garage. It gives me something to do—other than feeling sorry for myself. I turn it into a ritual, run fine white powder and flame over each salvaged piece to purify.

Phil comes out into the yard and signals over at me. "Another brake job just came in," he shouts. "You want it?"

I shake my head.

Phil hangs around anyway, but I refuse to turn back to him. The blowtorch ignites again, and I let the hissing wall of flame drown out anything he might say.

"A whole lot of them coming in recently," he yells over the noise.

"Yeah," I mumble through the mask. Yesterday a lady described her terror at hurtling full speed and realizing she couldn't stop. I wanted to tell her that being stuck in one place your whole life is just as scary.

"What are you making?" Phil says, walking closer to me, unfazed by the blowtorch.

"I don't know." I lift my mask. It's true. I don't. It sounds silly, but the objects just began telling me what shape they should take, what they wanted to be. I'm not about to tell Phil that.

"That college girl got to you," he says. I don't say anything, because it's not even a question. I would thank him for stating the fucking obvious, but I can't even trust my voice to hold steady.

I pick up my hammer and begin to tap at the pipe I've just incinerated.

Phil kicks a rock on the ground. "I know what it's like," he says.

Does he? I wonder. Does he know what it's like to feel yourself opening to possibility, only to be completely shut down. To dream of someone, only to realize you really were dreaming—you're as low as you thought.

"No one ever listens. Keep your heart like a rock. Hard as this metal," he's saying, knocking on a warped fender I've got leaning against the shed, though there's something soft in his voice. "That's what you gotta do."

"And how's that working out for you?"

"Hey, don't take it out on me, Romeo," he says, throwing his arms in the air. Despite his protest, I can tell that stung. He never has gone out with anyone since Denise.

"Sorry," I grumble.

"You can't talk to girls like that. They're just too different."

I nod noncommittally, try to make him go away. Of course, he's probably right.

I turn back to my project and see that the torque converter could become a shoe, that the camshaft I've just heated is an arm. It occurs to me—I am building a metal man. It's thrilling, the creation. Fusing the unlikeliest pieces together to form something new. Here is something I can mold, I think, something I can change.

I try to concentrate on my metal man, but I'm not left in peace for long. Phil comes back out half an hour later.

"Hey," he says, "that college chick is here to see you."

"Tell her I'm not here," I say.

"I already told her you were." He's enjoying this now.

I'm reluctant to leave my sculpture, so promising and solid. I take off my mask, my gloves, and stand there for a minute. Then I go to the bathroom and run my hands under water. No matter how many times I do, I always feel residue still on them. I look in the mirror at myself—dirty, unhappy—and try to harden my heart.

"Hey," I say to her. She's standing in the doorway looking unsure, and despite my resolve, I think she looks beautiful.

"Hey," she says. "Why haven't you returned my calls?"

"Been busy," I say, picking up a nearby wrench as if to show her what busy looks like.

"For over a week? Are you mad at me?"

I shrug. "Why would I be mad at you?"

"I feel like I did something wrong." When I don't say anything she asks, "Were you upset when I asked if I could hang out at the garage?"

I feel all of the guys behind me looking at us. They too have tools in their hands, but I know they're not working. They are listening to every word.

"Let's take a walk, ok?" I don't know what to say to her, but I don't want to say anything with them watching.

"Look," I say, when we get a little ways down the block—we're in front of the McDonald's—"I think maybe we're just too different. It's not going to work out."

Her big eyes grow bigger.

"It's ok, no big deal," I say to her, as she had said to me that first night in bed. I try to say it convincingly, as I've been trying to say it to myself all week.

"But it is a big deal. I thought things were going so well with us," she says.

"Look, I don't need to be some college girl's project. You don't have to date me to get your assignment, alright? There are plenty of garages in this town. Go find some other grease monkey," I add. This last line feels wrong even to me.

"What?" she says. "Oh my god, it's not like that at all! What an idiot."

"Yeah, I'm an idiot," I say.

"No, not you, me!" she says. "Forget about the assignment. It's not important. I just wanted to…I don't know. I'm stupid."

"You're smart. Maybe too smart for me."

"Are you kidding?" she says. "I don't think sometimes. I don't think."

I don't say anything. I watch the cars pulling up to the drive-through. Each person leans their head out the window, straining to decipher what the squawking black box is saying.

"All anyone ever sees is the garage, like it's all I am."

"I know you're more than that. Do you know how smart you are? You think quick. You do things, you don't just talk." Emily looks like she's going to cry. "What do I do? Stay in school, one program after another, because I can't do anything real."

"Hey now, don't do that," I say, extending my arm, and it's not until I do that I realize I'm still holding my wrench. I pull her to my chest.

"This was my fault," she says, wiping her nose into my shirt. "But I think maybe there's something else. You're better than *you* think you are. Did you know that?"

We stand there for a moment as I watch the cars across the street stop, start, stop, start. They talk into the talking box, then pick up their food at the glass window. After that, they take off in one of two directions.

"So where do we go from here?" I ask.

"From now on, you decide," she says.

I don't say anything for awhile, then draw her closer to me again, let myself lay my chin on the top of her head. "Yeah," I say. "It's time for a change.

At closing time, I let the boys go ahead of me; I say I'll close up shop. I turn the lights out in the garage, leaving behind the ailing cars in all manner of state—some flying high in the air on blocks, others parked inert on the ground. I'm not sure if it's something to be proud of, but there are none I can't fix.

I go out back and look at the sculpture I've been working on all week. It was all old scrap before, but it's really becoming something now. Maybe I'll tell Emily about it, though maybe it's just for me. To know there's a temperature at which metal begins to bend, and that when it does, you can shape it into anything.

Rebecca Thomas

Spring Training

F rancisco Romero caught a glimpse of her before she disappeared
down his street. In his living room, he sat reading the morning's paper
and sensed that someone was watching. His eyes left the news about the
Angels' trade—an outfielder, useless; they needed a second baseman—
and shifted to his window. He saw her staring at his boarded-up home as
she walked away, and he watched her for as long as the window let him,
following her as she passed the vacant dirt lot next door. She kept glancing back as she walked, and he wondered if his house had been tagged
somehow and he didn't know it, that he was losing his sixth sense for graf-
fiti. But then she showed up again, the sleeves of her striped button-up
rolled to her elbows, her red hair pulled tight into a ponytail, and he knew.
She had come for his land.

On the radio, NPR listed the day's horrors and advertised upcoming
entertainment. She knocked, and he opened his real door first, the oak
one that his parents brought from Mexico, before opening a plywood
door, cheaper, and sturdier, than a screen.

"Good afternoon," she said. The woman was young, younger than
thirty, younger even than his youngest. He waited. He wasn't going to
make this easy. She scratched behind her ear and asked, "How are you?"

"They make you work on a Saturday, huh?" he said.

She smiled and waved her hand as if she was shooing a fly. "I'm here
from—"

"I'm not selling."

"I think if you just—"

"Tell your employers," at this he pointed down the street towards the private university two blocks away. "Tell them that they can wait until I die. I have two boys who will be happy to sell, then." He smoothed his flannel shirt before rubbing his hands on his faded jeans.

The woman coughed and turned it into a laugh.

He leaned forward, smiling. "This has nothing to do with you, but I'm going to shut the door in your face. You have a nice day." He nodded and closed the doors.

She knocked. He didn't answer. His footsteps creaked on the wooden floors as he walked across the living room and turned up the radio, letting other people's car problems flood his house. She didn't go away until this week's puzzler halfway through the hour-long show.

That next week, pitchers and catchers reported. They were the only good thing the Angels had going for them. He liked saying their names out loud as he read about the week's progress. It centered him, like the rosary.

His car inched along the 57 Freeway, snaking through the foothills of Brea, and he listened for news about his team on his drive to and from Cal Poly. He taught mathematics at the university. On the way back, the radio reported that one of the Angels' starting pitchers injured his wrist while walking his dog in Arizona. He tripped on a curb, got tangled up in the leash, and fell on the street. Fractured. "Over a year to recover," the reporter said. "With surgery."

"There goes the season," Francisco said. Over before it started. He checked the time. His oldest would still be at work, but his youngest, Alberto, lived in Chicago. He'd be free. He called him. "You hear the news?" he asked, and they chatted about the Angels' chances this season, but there's only so much pre-season speculation, and when the conversation lulled, Francisco cleared his throat and said, "The school came around again."

"Makes sense," Alberto said. "It's a good spot and a big lot. Why wouldn't they?"

"They sent someone out this time."

"Change of strategy it seems. You going to sell?"

"Of course not."

"You should think about it, Dad. All growing up, you complained about that place to Mom, and now you won't get rid of it."

"It's part of the family."

"It's a dump."

"It's just old."

"If you aren't going to sell, at least consider letting us fix it up a bit."

"I don't need your help with that," Francisco said. "I can afford it, you know."

"I know," Alberto said. "I was just offering my time, but it would just be good to see you doing something with the place. Nothing's changed since grandma passed."

Daisies bloomed in the emergency lane, a burst of yellow amongst the icicle plants. Francisco cleared his throat. "How's the baby?" he asked.

"Alice is doing well," Alberto said, stressing the name. Francisco stared at the car ahead of him. Alberto named his baby after his mother, and Francisco liked that, this tribute, but he still had a hard time hearing his wife's name even if it had been six years ago. "It'd be nice if you said her name, you know," Alberto said.

"It's a beautiful name for a beautiful baby girl." Francisco ran his hands along the steering wheel. "So come on, give me baby updates." He let Alberto talk for the rest of the time.

On Saturday, Francisco sat in his easy chair reading about the players' conditioning. A ceiling fan pushed air from exposed wooden rafters. The sun that slinked in from the cracks in the windows and under the door whispered of heat. The house wasn't stuffy yet, but it was bound to reach past eighty.

Someone knocked. He jumped. And there she was, smiling, as he opened the door. Heat rushed in, settling around his slippered feet.

"Atlanta, Georgia. Seven a.m.," she said. Her hair was down this time, bright red, frizzy. Freckles polka-dotted her body.

"What?"

"The answer to last week's puzzler." She pointed to the sound of the radio.

"Okay." He stepped forward to take the door from her.

"My name is April."

"Francisco." Letting go of the door, he stuck out his hand. She took it. They shook, and he let go, rubbing his hands on his navy pants, clapping them together once before grasping them to keep them still.

"Nice to meet you," she said.

He moved to the plywood door, trying to pull it closed, but April didn't let go. "So, you like Car Talk?" she asked.

Francisco nodded.

"I don't miss a week."

"Me either," he said. "Until baseball season." He tried the door again, but she held on.

"Never could get into baseball, but cars…" She nodded to the driveway. A tan hatchback covered in sunspots and hub-cap-less. "That was my first."

"Really?" Francisco let go of the door.

"It was five years old when I had it almost ten years ago, but I loved it. Transmission go out on you yet? That's what finally did mine in." Francisco nodded. "Yeah, but I replaced it. I'm on my fifth timing belt, too."

"I was on my third." April smiled. "I miss it, though. It was sturdy." Francisco looked down at his feet. "It's a good car. Raised my boys in it. Taught them both to drive in it."

"I can see why you'd keep it, then," April said. "But your fifth timing belt?" She shook her head. "That's impressive."

He shrugged. "It runs. My boys want me to get something new, offered to pay for it." He rolled his eyes. "Like that would make me change my mind. But it works. There's no sense in showing off with something new."

April smiled. "Showing off? There's a difference between showing off and being stubborn if you ask me."

"I didn't."

April held up her hands. "You're right." She rummaged through her purse and pulled out a letter. "We're trying a different approach this time, Mr. Romero. Hand-delivered letters."

"Just to let you know, I'm throwing this away. It's best to be up front about these things, not waste anybody's time."

April let go of the plywood door and patted the house's patchy stucco walls. Mercado Romero faintly peeked through the layers of tan paint, as did the endless repetition of the local gang's symbol—OCAX3. "If I'm not going to waste anyone's time, if you're refusing to listen to me…" She waited. He said nothing. "I guess I should just get going, Mr. Romero."

"Frank."

"Fine then, Frank, read the letter. We'll talk. We'd really love this property. We'll take good care of it." She walked down the street, passing the dirt lot. Kids played soccer. She glanced at them before continuing.

Frank stepped out of his house, his slippered feet resting on his threshold.

She turned around. "See you," she said and kept on walking.

He stood for a moment, his eyes scanning his block. So much had changed since he was a boy. Even still, two years after his mother passed, it seemed strange to be back, to be the owner of this plot of land that he couldn't wait to escape as a child.

The boys played soccer next to him, running up and down the dirt that had once been his parents' garden. As a boy, he used to plant with his mother each season, squatting next to her, mixing up the soil, feeling the earth for rocks, marveling at the worms that hid below his feet. Together, they'd plant peas and greens in the fall, tomatoes and beans in the spring, peppers. He'd push the seeds under the ground, the dirt caking under his fingernails, filling the lines of his palms. In the morning before the sun baked the top of the earth dry and cracked like a loaf of bread, they'd water and watch for signs of life. He learned patience, then, the seedlings always taking longer than he anticipated, always waiting for him to tell his mother, "I guess they're a bad batch. We should start over," until the seeds sprouted like they needed him to stop believing in them before they could germinate. Then they would, sprinting with each other until everything towered over the boy, until the beans grew tall enough for him to sit under and read. But he grew up, and his Alice did the planting at their house until she passed. When Frank moved back home to take care of his mother, she was too old to plant, and she wouldn't have remembered to water. And then, she passed away, too.

Now, kids played there during the daytime and older ones sold stuff at night. Looking at his land, he could practically see the parking lot that the university would build once his boys sold. It was only a matter of time.

Banjo music spilled from his house, the theme song for the car show. He went back inside, put the letter in his back pocket, and did dishes while the brothers talked car repair. He let the water run loud during this week's puzzler, but his ears still reached to hear the answer. She had been right.

On Monday, he thought about April as he drove to work. He thought of the letter, open and resting on the top of his desk at home. He thought of the puzzler that week. He had tried to drown out the question, but his ears still caught most of it, and as he sat in traffic, his mind returned to it again and again. He checked the time. His oldest would still be at home. He called.

"I have a riddle for you," Frank said.

"I've got to go to work, Dad," Frank Jr. said. He went by Francisco, but Frank refused, calling him Frankie, Junior, or Francisco Xavier Junior Romero when he was pissed.

"Come on. Listen. Help me with it."

Frank Jr. sighed. "Fine."

Frank repeated the riddle and the two men discussed options. Frank could hear his son scratch out the math on a pad of paper.

"I'm stuck," Frank Jr. said.

"Get unstuck. You're the math genius."

"You're the professor," his son said. "What does it matter?"

"It doesn't."

"Well that's some bullshit."

"Language."

"Don't language me."

Frank scrunched his face, craned his neck around him. He was surrounded by semis. He needed to get over one lane to avoid the 91 Interchange traffic. He waited for an open spot.

"I talked to Alberto," Frank Jr. said. "Someone stopped by?"

"Doesn't matter."

"Why don't you just talk to her, Dad? What could be so wrong with that?"

"She won't listen. She's a pest."

"She's just doing her job. She's probably nice."

"You would say that."

The semis sat next to and in front of him. His hatchback barely coming to the trucks' wheels.

"She does listen to Car Talk," Frank said. "Or it could be a ploy."

"Everything's not a ploy, Dad." His son cleared his throat. "I started seeds indoors this week. Put a few peppers by that window that gets the afternoon sun. We'll see what happens."

"Right," Frank said. "Good. Family tradition and all that."

"Dad?" his son asked. He paused, but Frank said nothing. "Dad?"

"I'm fine," Frank said. "Don't worry."

The hills burst green, a deep green, one that came from winter rains, not sprinklers. It shifted in the breeze. There, sitting in the number two lane, the hills made him feel as if there was enough water. It let him forget the drought PSAs and his own patch of dirt, already cracked from the sun. He looked over his left shoulder, saw that he had enough space, and got over.

On Saturday, he tried to read the paper. Players were starting to report, converging in Arizona. He read about the injury. Nothing new. Nothing good. He turned down the radio. Checked his watch. Listened for her.

He kept his back to the window, making himself stare ahead and away from the door. But his ears strained. He checked his watch again. She was late.

He heard her footsteps.

He opened the door before she had a chance to knock. "Did you hear the call with the woman and the bad brakes?"

"Did you think about the letter?"

"She couldn't figure out what the screeching was, right. Eeeee! Eeeee!" Frank imitated the sound of the caller. "Like a dolphin." Frank let go of the door, leaned against it, his shoulder resting on the wooden frame. "What kind of person doesn't know the sound of bad brakes?"

"I brought some paperwork for you."

Frank moved his feet back on his side of the threshold. He waved her off. "What about the puzzler? You know the answer's twenty-four," he began.

She smiled. "Thirty-seven."

"Sixty-two," they said together and then laughed.

"Did you hear the one about—" Frank began.

April stepped forward, her patent leather flats resting on his wood floor. "Did you read the letter?"

"Yeah. Yeah. Very generous. Now, about the caller…"

"So, you have nothing to say about our offer?"

Frank shrugged. "I've heard it before."

"This is more generous."

"It's still taking my house, so, no. Now, what about the guy who only bought gas in the morning?"

April leaned against the doorframe. "I'm here to do my job, Frank."

"Well, no one asked you."

"Can you just tell me why you want to keep this place so badly?"

"It's my home," he said. "Now, this guy called—"

"Frank—"

"Let's not talk about it."

"You can't just listen? I'll leave you alone if you listen."

Frank waved her off. "I've heard it before. Now—"

"Now what?" April took a step forward. Only her heels rested on the threshold. Everything else was inside Frank's house. "You turn me away. You talk about the car show, but you won't even answer my question? Do you like living here?"

"Of course, it's my home. This is where I'm from." He looked down at her feet. Raised his eyebrows.

She looked down at her feet, raised her eyebrows, too, stayed. "We want your land. You know this. I know that you don't want to sell. I just want to know why, honestly. Are we wasting our time?" She patted the piebald walls. "I look around, and I don't know. I just want to talk."

Frank stepped forward. "Well, I'm not talking about that."

"Fine, then, I'll go."

"We haven't even talked about the woman who found a cat in her car."

"What are you doing here, Frank?"

Frank felt the heat rush to his ears. "You wouldn't respect this place."

She nodded to the dirt lot. "Tell me how you're respecting this place."

"What the hell does that mean?"

"You want to talk respect? Let's talk respect." She looked over at the dirt lot. Frank followed her stare. Some kids had left their bag of flaming hot Cheetos in the middle of it. "This doesn't look like the home of some-one who enjoys living here. This looks house looks abandoned. It's boarded up. There's weeds. You have chicken wire over the window."

"You know nothing about my house," he jabbed at his chest, "about my land." He shook his head. "You spend your days over in that fantasyland. You all act like you own this town, but you know nothing about it."

April stepped back. She took a breath. "You are standing in the Mercado Romero. Your mother and father operated it until 1985. Over there," she pointed across the dirt lot to the mission-like house, "is the community center built by Methodists in 1915. It served as the center until the late Seventies. The owner now rents it and makes more money than my school can offer. There," she pointed behind her to the giant parking structure one block away, "was where the school was for the packing-house kids. Segregated until World War II. Torn down in 1998 by my school."

"So what? You've done your homework."

"I grew up here. I live a block away. I watched this neighborhood change. I bought Orange Crush and Its-It bars from your parents, Frank. I know about this neighborhood, okay?"

"And still—"

"It's a job, Frank. I took what I could get." He started to speak. She held up her hand. "I know what I'm asking. But look, what message are you sending the neighborhood? To the city?" She pointed to the dirt, to the boarded up windows, to the wall quilted in shades of tan paint. "This place looks abandoned. You don't even do anything with the lot like your parents. Is it any wonder we keep bugging you to sell?"

Frank's arms shook. "If you come next week, I'll call the cops."

"I'm just doing my job, Mr. Romero."

"I'll call your boss. Report you."

"Call my boss, please." April held up her hands. "He's the one that put me on this assignment. He said I had an 'in.'" April took hold of the door and began to push it shut, making Frank step back to get out of the way.

But Frank caught the door, his fingers above hers. "Your in is bullshit. If you really understood this place, you wouldn't work for them."

"This job has benefits, a salary."

"You sold yourself to them. If you come back, I'll get you fired."

"You are a lonely man, Frank." April held up her hands. "Fine. You win. Enjoy your land, sir. You're doing a hell of a job." She swept out her hands, motioning to the lake of dirt, and walked away.

Frank waited to find something to say, but his mind only sent down images to him—his mother in her favorite purple dress, his boys picking tomatoes with Alice in their backyard, himself under the bean vines as a boy. He had just finished *Huckleberry Finn,* and he fashioned himself a raft with the discarded lemon pallets from the packinghouse, using the bean vines as twine. On the days when the other kids went to the city pool, he pulled out his raft and pretended.

The boys played soccer all that day, the ball hitting his wall every few minutes, rattling a family portrait that had hung there since he was a boy. He remembered that picture, taken at a photo studio on the block back when businesses still dotted the street. It had been August, and it was over a hundred, but his mother made him wear his church suit and white button-up and tie. Sweat covered his face, and she put a fedora on him to hide his soaked hair and forehead. His brother, somehow, had been able to stay fedora free. As the photographer posed the boys, Frank looked over at Alex and, seeing Alex's sweat-free face, momentarily despised him.

The soccer ball hit the wall again. April didn't know about this place, he thought. If she did, she would've realized that this was the best place those boys could play within walking distance. He looked out the kitchen door's window to the spot behind his house where the kids never played, where his mother's garden had started, small at first before it covered the entire yard. Seed catalogs still came each winter, each page promising summer, but he could never bring himself to order. Besides, he thought, even if he did get the seeds, he wasn't the gardener. They were, and they were gone. And April knew none of that, he thought. She knew nothing.

He looked up her information. Her office number. Her boss. Her job title. He called several times, waiting for the machine to kick in, before hanging up at the beep, not knowing what to say.

On Monday, he called his work, coughed into the phone, and said that he'd need to cancel his classes that day. He was sick.

He worked out what he was going to say. She was belligerent, abusive, rude, insulting. She should be fired. He said this to himself as he got dressed, putting on his best Orange County clothes—khakis and a Tommy Bahamas shirt—and walked the two blocks to the university's administration offices. The building was small, a one story stucco rectangle, covered in ivy to age it. He walked along the carpeted floor, passing alcove after alcove of administrative positions until he found the purchasing department. A woman looked up. "Yes?" she asked.

"I'd like to speak to Todd," he said.

"Do you have an—"

"No." He smoothed his khakis and patted his silken Hawaiian shirt. "I live down the street and wanted to discuss the matter of selling my house."

The woman smiled, told him to wait. She popped out for a few minutes before ushering Frank back.

But April was there, standing by the coffee machine in the hall. She stopped, her red hair even brighter against the white walls.

Frank stepped back.

"You came to my work?" she asked.

He stepped back again. "I—"

But Todd Mackleroy walked out of his office, looking like the picture of an Orange County businessman—white, Ken-doll brown hair, shirt sleeves rolled up. He offered a meaty hand to Frank. "Francisco," he said.

"Todd."

Frank shook his hand, his eyes still on April.

Todd walked over and patted her on the shoulder before catching himself and taking a step back. "Nice work," he said. "Never thought we'd catch this guy."

April laughed, high, nervous, like a chipmunk.

Frank took another step back, but Todd walked to him and ushered him into his office—a study in mahogany. A Beach Boys–signed picture framed behind his desk. "April," he called out. "Get in on this action." He turned to Frank. "Sit, please." He sat down behind the desk.

Frank heard April's heels thud against the carpet behind him, but he wouldn't look around. "Yes, Frank, sit," she said, her voice calm. "Be comfortable."

Todd stared at April, his eyebrows raised, but Frank didn't turn around. "Come on, April," Todd said, "you can do a better welcome than that."

April cleared her throat, and Frank felt her hands on his shoulders, squeezing him. "So good to see you, Frank." She patted him twice, hard. "Let's chat." When she sat in the chair next to him, he had to look at her. She grinned, but there was fear in her eyes.

Frank stayed standing. His hands clutched the burgundy leather chair. "Yes, well." He peeked at April. He thought of his wife; he knew what she'd say about this. "I'm not selling my home. I won't sell it. I can't. Thanks, though." He nodded twice, eyes on the ground and not on April or Todd, before leaving. He heard Todd's voice. He knew Todd was asking him a question, but he didn't turn around. He just kept walking home.

The hills stayed green that week. The land held its breath as heat waves threatened, reaching eighty degrees but never any higher. Frank watched the hills as he drove to work, waiting for the moment when the grasses browned and turned into matches. He'd do this each year—watch the land during spring as it greened itself, and he would think inevitably of his wife and his mother and the ground all brown and dried up. And each year, spring passed quickly, the wildflowers dead before baseball season was even a month in. This year, he knew, would be no different. But for now, the grass stayed. It soothed him even when his pulse quickened at commercials for the car show, but he kept his eyes on the hills, making himself think about the idea that spring could linger.

That Saturday, the car show played on his radio. He waited for her to show up so they could talk, but after the first three callers, he realized that she wasn't going to. He was just wasting his time waiting, he thought, and he got in his car and drove to the Home Depot while people described their problems on the radio. He parked and went inside.

He missed the answer to the puzzler. He was standing in front of the garden section when the brothers made the announcement. He grabbed a shovel, a hoe, and a rake before finding the wall of seeds. He studied their pictures, considered their promises of drought and pest resistance, of heirloom taste.

At home, he worked the land behind his house as the radio played.

He marked out a plot of dirt, making sure to leave space for the boys to play soccer. He switched the radio to the first spring training game of the season as he broke up the clay earth. He dumped out bag after bag of soil and compost and listened for names, for balls and strikes and double-plays, for the sound of bat on ball, listening to the rhythm of the game until he forgot that he was working. Then, it was just the weight of earth against rake, the sound of baseball. Spring.

A group of boys stopped by to play soccer and see what he was doing. All but one left. The boy, no older than eight, stared at the ground and at Frank, until Frank asked if he wanted to help. The boy nodded, and the two squatted together as they dropped beans into neat rows—Rattlesnake, Fortex, Kentucky Wonder Wax. The boy patted the soil down after Frank dropped in a seed. They watered as the sun brushed the horizon. When they were finished, the boy asked what came next. "We wait," Frank said. "They'll come, grow, and then, we eat."

Shelly Rodrigue

The Fisherman's Son

Swearing suited him, the captain
of the trawler, *Silver Spoon*.
Just like his father, the skipper of the *Bender Rover*.

Reluctant in telling the vessels' origins, modest
in both mind and money, but never mouth,
teaching me phrases like *fuck that noise* and
celery is for rabbits and goddamn Californians.

You'd never guess he was an engineer and a gentleman
or he didn't stink of Bristol Bay under that seldom beard
with eyes bluer than the waters on which he sailed
and sunny, blond hair drunken with excess daylight or
how every summer I missed him.

He told me the story of Einer Landstetter, Norwegian
badass, and how *if given enough time, a man will
work his way out of his own problems,*
how that sentiment almost killed his own father,
and sometimes that was the best way to make a friend.

He told me about another man, who, in a drug-induced psychosis
ran naked through Nanek pressing his grimy body against
restaurant windows because he believed no one could see him,
and *that was the second time he went invisible!*

Unwilling or unable to tell me about the first,
and declining to change his shirt in my presence
because *what woman wants to be forced to see a naked man?*

And the name, Dirty Mike, because every hitchhiking
prostitute in Alaska asked him, the lone truck driver,
for a ride, never disclosing whether or not he obliged,
except for the time he didn't sleep with her.

He told me many things in the seasons of inebriation,
of alcoholic, olive-oil foot massages, of him—
fisherman against his good mother's wishes,
a clean-shaven homeschooled kid
prevented from *Mass. Maritime* by one
dirt-bike broken leg.

Summers were for fishing salmon:
a time for men to go and be men.

But summers, oh, those sobering summers, I still spent
at the beck and call of a glass of gin.

Angela Nishimoto

Sex Education:
A Tragicomedy
of Seven Years

Romance (A)

When I was six years old, my parents had a Nichiren Shoshu of America church meeting at our home. Members from all over O'ahu's windward side descended on our little house in Kāne'ohe on Uhilehua Street. The grown-ups chanted the liturgy, sang, recounted experiences, and vowed to practice harder.

Many of the children were outside the brightly lit house, playing in the cul-de-sac, running around in the dark. I walked on the coral-chip path at the front of our place, sounds of the meeting filling my ears. Rickie Ching, a boy from an area north of Kahalu'u, sauntered up to me and put his arm around my shoulders.

"We go kiss," he commanded.

I brushed my long hair away from my face and puckered up.

He planted a big, fat, wet one on my tightly pursed lips.

"You wen' like 'em?" he demanded.

"Yeth," I said. I drew the back of my hand across my lips.

He took my hand and we walked to the front door. He put his hand on the back of my neck to kiss me again, but I exhaled through my mouth on his face.

"Whoa!" he said. "Your breat' stink!"

I pressed my lips together, over my decayed front teeth—gotten from jumping on the bed and falling face-first onto the cold, tiled floor of my bedroom.

He flung my hand away and stomped off into the house.

I stayed behind, kicking at the coral chips like I wanted to kick at his 'ōkole.

Romance (B)

Regan was as small as I was, and in my third-grade class at Kapunahala Elementary School. We were in Japanese school together, too. I figured we were a match. He'd run up to me and punch me hard in the upper arm, his bony knuckles hurting me, then run away, me giving chase. Sometimes he'd chase me. He reminded me of my father.

During recess one day, Regan and Jason and I were running, chasing each other. I screamed and ran into the girls' bathroom in the squat cream-painted building that housed the first-grade classrooms.

"Eh!" Regan yelled, his voice echoing off the pink tiles. "I'm gonna get you! Jus' wait!"

I hung back for what seemed like forever. Then, deciding that they'd lost interest, I edged out onto the walkway. The way was open. I trotted to the end of the building towards the playground, rounded the corner, and spied the two boys throwing rocks at a small plumeria tree in the grassy area between the buildings.

I ran up to Regan and hit him on the back, making him sway forward, then turned to flee. But he caught my wrist. Jason got my other arm. They pulled on me. Yanked side to side, I sank my long fingernails into Regan's arm as hard as I could.

"Ow!" His small eyes narrowed. "You suckin' Angela!" He knocked my legs out from under me with his right leg. Between the two boys, I flopped again and again. Jason seemed uneasy. But Regan's eyes were intent, the thin lips of his little mouth compressed and determined.

Jason let me go, but Regan put both his hands on my arm and swung me around. I kicked at him, scared into silence. He was so angry.

"We go!" Jason said. The bell rang.

Regan was breathing hard, kicking at me. Then he pushed me down, kicked me once more, and the two boys ran off.

At Sea

Kāneʻohe Bay. A man took us out on his boat. The bay was choppy. The waves were like peaks in the mountains, but these were small and dark blue with frothy white caps. The boat rocked.

It smelled fresh, of ozone, fresh like clean water. The white boat churned across the surface by its propellers. We children were quiet, too—in apprehension? But the boat moved, the waves making their lapping, sucking noises against the boat. I heard birds and the drone of the motor, but no voices. The sky was leaden, no sun.

We shivered. The wind on the bay chilled our faces. We wore jackets, but we were still cold. Steering the boat, the man didn't talk. Was he angry? He was a quiet, unsmiling man, though handsome, with black, curly hair. His eyes had heavy lids; his lips were full, too. His eyes were dark and open, looking at the water.

It was my first time on a boat, and the shore looked so far away. Though my sister Wendy and brother, Mark, were there, too, I wasn't very aware of them. We were here with this silent man, a stranger who didn't smile or act friendly, like many adults did when they were with children.

Our father never explained anything to us, so this outing was a mystery, like so much of our lives. My father is quiet, especially when he's angry—and he's angry much of the time. But he'd seemed happy earlier, when he was giving the stranger money. I'd hung back, thinking, He's only fooling, right? He's not going to make us go away on a boat with a stranger, right?

Or did the man give Daddy money for us? Did we belong to him now? Could he do anything he wanted to us—like yell and hit us and tell us to shut up when we cried? The waves made noise, the motor made noise. I didn't quite articulate the word kidnap to myself, but I was worried about that, too.

Did Daddy give us away like unwanted puppies? Or would this silent man take us away and drown us like kittens? Time didn't exist—the waves lapping, the dark, dark sea so big. The boat creaked. And sometimes there was the cry of a bird, like a lost soul. The wind tasted of salt. The air tasted of sea. I was uncharacteristically quiet.

Usually quiet, both my sister and brother seemed all right. But I was usually noisy. "You rascal!" my father would say to me, ruffling my hair when he was in a good mood. "You monkey!"

The man anchored the boat on the sandbar. Wendy and Mark stripped to their swimsuits and jumped off the boat through the low-tide shallow water onto the white sand. They yelled and laughed at the coldness of the water, splashing each other.

"Go play," the man said, but I shook my head, my arms hugging myself. What if he motored the boat away, leaving us on the sandbar? How could we get back home? As the oldest, I was responsible.

He drew something up: a trap with five or six crabs, greenish black, glistening from the water. The bodies, the black, shiny bodies of the crabs moved, the mass writhing in the basket. The quiet man reached in and grabbed a moving crab and broke off a leg. He sucked at the leg, holding the rest of the crab in his other hand, its other legs waving. The wind was cold. I was hypnotized by the hapless crab, so silent, its legs waving so helplessly.

The man broke off another leg and held it out to me, and I took it and tried to do the same, feeling the cold, crusty leg against my lips, my tongue. I sucked out its meat, surprised at its sashimi taste, something familiar in this strange place with this stranger. The salty water, the fishy leg. I tried not to watch the crab waving its doomed limbs around. I tried not to imagine the agony of someone pulling my leg off and eating it while I was still alive. The man pulled off leg after leg and sucked them dry, tossing the empty legs into the water. He broke off the last leg, put it into his mouth, and threw the limbless torso into the sea. I watched it sink, bubbles rising, as the man put his hand on my shoulder.

My father was happy about giving money to the stranger to take us away. Years later, I realized that he and my mother had some private time together that day, with only baby Julie to watch. And that outing had been meant to be fun for us. But no one had told me.

To & From King

We went to King Intermediate School from Kapunahala Elementary, to the seventh grade. The first day of school, we got off the school bus in front of King, and I heard a girl say from the second floor of the building, "They look so small."

On the way to King on the shoulder-to-shoulder crowded bus, the driver would sometimes yell at us, *Shut up!*

My friend Lynne said to a boy, "How come you hogging one whole seat?"

He was sitting with both legs sticking into the aisle. He grinned at her, slid to the middle of the seat, and spread his legs. He patted the space in front of his crotch and said, "Come then! We go ff-ff!"

She pulled her mouth into an unhappy crooked line. The bus braked, and people standing jerked towards the rear.

On the way home, the bus driver's neck was red. *Move to the rear of the bus!* he shouted. He braked hard.

Those of us standing jerked backwards again, and someone grabbed me by the crotch, under my short skirt. I looked around, but couldn't tell who'd done it.

Our group of seven or eight small girls started walking to and from King every school day all the way from Keapuka, a one-way walk of three miles. Then we broke up into groups of twos and threes with our long, middle-parted hair and our shorts or short skirts with tops. "Too crowded, on the bus," one of the girls said, grimacing.

Who wears short-shorts? the long-legged lovelies on TV sang. They never seemed to have problems with boys grabbing them when they were off-balance.

By the time of the rainy season in Kāneʻohe, my mom was driving Willow and me to school before work. We'd leave the house at 6:15. My friend and I would hang around, holding our books in front, or pace the walkways until homeroom at 8.

Un-Steadied

Since we'd been in the sixth grade, couples would go steady. I'd never had a steady. I started wearing eye makeup and lip gloss when I was twelve. I sewed most of my dresses, having taken a summer sewing class. I mostly wore short dresses or Hang Ten tee-shirts and shorts. I was a small girl and had read in *Seventeen* that if you were petite, you should wear short skirts. It was also the time of the miniskirt—the early 1970s.

At the beginning of eighth grade, Liesel came up to me, standing on the walkway with some friends, and said, "Robert wants to know if he get chance."

Surprised, I thought it over. Then I noticed that Liesel was looking at me narrow eyed and thin lipped. I hastily said, "No."

She smiled and said, "Okay. I'll tell him." She walked away.

Then I remembered that Robert and Liesel had gone together.

The next week, Ken asked me, "Lyle get chance?"

Thinking about it, I decided that I didn't want to be unfair to Robert. So I said, "No."

Nobody asked me again after that.

Gerda Govine Ituarte

Two Poems

Veteran

Enters room	presence spreads	sits carefully
weight of what was	captures air	breath breaks
eyes glaze	split second fade	blinks back
body bears scars	metal plates hold	wonder why
climb out of fog	dreams unfurl	nail to ground.

I Love When

He's in paint mode.

      Colors come out to play.

Red   Orange

      Blue   Purple

        Yellow   Green

Stands close to canvas

      almost cross eyed.

Takes step back, forward,

      sips coffee,

      stares intently,

      2nd, 3rd, 4th round.

      Defining

           Refining

             Crafting

Do you think I'm finished?
Do you think you're finished?

Amy Holwerda

Gardenia

Saul sat almost peacefully staring at the aquarium in the waiting room, watching the neon fish cut their way through the water. When the blonde nurse entered the room, Saul wanted to tell her to sit down. Pour herself a cup of coffee. He knew what she was going to say, and that he wouldn't be able to stop her. He swallowed hard and nodded.

"I'm so sorry, Mr. Huber," she said.

Saul didn't want to look the girl in the eyes. She was young. Too young, he thought, to be dealing with death.

The nurse's bright pink fingernails clicked against her clipboard as she flipped through pages. "We called your daughter. She should be here in an hour. Would you like to sit with your wife while you wait?" The thought of sitting in the room with Henrietta's dead body made Saul's eyes glaze over. A heavy weight pooled in his chest. "Like the doctor said, she went peacefully," the nurse said. Saul wondered why she was smiling. "In her sleep. There wasn't any pain."

"Please leave," Saul said.

The clipboard sagged in the nurse's hands. She stopped at the doorway. "I'm so sorry for your loss," she said, but the words sounded like tin.

When the nurse was gone, Saul sat and listened to the clock ticking away seconds behind him. He shouldn't have snapped at her, he thought. It wasn't her fault Henrietta died. But he didn't want to face that room, didn't want to see her lying beneath a white sheet. He would wait until his daughter, Emily, arrived. He rose from the chair and shuffled out to the hallway. A group of nurses huddled around a desk, whispering. One pointed in his direction.

"Excuse me," he said. "Could one of you please call my daughter? She'll have to drive in from Michigan."

The blonde nurse blinked. "Call her again?"

She looked familiar, but Saul couldn't place her. "My daughter Emily," he said. "She lives in Michigan."

The nurses exchanged glances. "She's on her way, sir," the blonde nurse said, running bright pink nails through her hair. "I called her a few minutes ago."

Saul remembered. He shook his head. "That's right," he said. "I was just making sure."

Before she died, Henrietta had been sleeping poorly. She woke in the middle of the night, struggling for breath. "It feels like someone's squeezing shut my windpipe," she said. Saul urged her to call the doctor. "Nonsense," she said. "It's just apnea. It'll pass."

But Saul wasn't convinced. He crept out of bed while Henrietta slept and wrote down her symptoms in a green notebook. He wrote down what he wanted to tell the doctor and practiced the conversation in the mirror so he wouldn't forget anything. Even so, the doctor sounded nonplussed. "Give it a few days, Mr. Huber," he said. "If she still can't sleep or if her symptoms escalate, have her come in and see me, okay?" Saul wrote down everything the doctor said and promised he would follow his instructions. When Henrietta came home from her knitting class that day, she showed Saul the progress she made on the baby blanket she was knitting. "Never know when this might come in handy," she said, even though their only child, Emily, was thirty-eight and unmarried. Saul nodded and wrote it down in his notebook: *Baby blanket for Emily*.

On the day of Henrietta's attack, she and Saul were shopping for groceries for their weekly card game. On Sunday nights, they hosted a game of gin rummy and a group of friends came over at seven to play. When Saul began forgetting the rules of the game he wanted to call off the parties, but Henrietta wouldn't hear of it. Each week she patiently went over the rules, even the weeks he didn't need to be reminded. If he started to panic halfway through a game, Henrietta could tell by the way he stared wildly at the cards. "Saul, why don't you help me refill this cheese plate," she would say. In the kitchen, she whispered the rules in his ear. "Nobody has to know," she said.

At the grocery store, they had gathered their purchases and were making their way back to the car when Henrietta stopped short. Saul turned around, and she was shaking her left arm, as if trying to restore circulation.

"Damn," she said. "Damn my arm."

"Everything okay?" Saul shouted.

When Henrietta looked up, her face had gone white and sweaty. "Growing pains," she said weakly. Saul dropped the grocery bags and hurried back. When he reached her, Henrietta had slumped down to the ground, hand clutched at her chest. "I can't breathe, Saul," she said.

"Help," Saul shouted to the gathering crowd. "We need help!"

An ambulance was there in minutes. Henrietta's eyes rolled back in her head, eyelashes fluttering. "Oh, Henny," Saul said. He patted her cheek with a shaking hand.

One of the EMTs elbowed his way between them. "Sir, are you riding along?"

Saul watched the workers strap Henrietta to a backboard and load her onto the rig. He thought of the questions he might be asked. About her medical history, the pills she was taking. He wasn't sure if he could remember the answers. What if he answered a question wrong? Through the tiny back window of the ambulance, he could see someone compressing Henrietta's chest. The siren screamed on. "I'm sorry sir, we need to move," the worker said. Saul watched as the flashing lights disappeared.

Tests revealed that Henrietta had underlying arteriosclerosis coronary heart disease.

"What does that mean," Saul asked.

"It's a general term," the doctor said, glancing down at Henrietta's chart. "It means that the walls of your wife's heart have thickened with fat. One of these sacs of fat broke away, clotting blood flow in Henrietta's heart, causing the attack."

"Please, I need you to write it down," Saul said. "I forget things some-times."

"We'll have to watch her closely," the doctor said. "In situations like this it's not uncommon for patients to have repeated attacks."

When the doctor was gone, Saul rested his hand on Henrietta's shoul-der. "I'm going to tell Emily," he said. "What if I can't take care of you?"

Henrietta's voice sounded tired but determined. "We're the parents," she said. "We take care of her."

"I don't know what I'll do without you," he wanted to say, but his throat clenched. He had never been one to cry and couldn't bear the thought of Henrietta seeing his weakness, not now when she needed him to be strong.

"I'm not going anywhere," she said. Then she placed the oxygen mask back over her mouth and patted his hands before she closed her eyes. Saul sat next to her bed, wringing his hands, watching her fall asleep.

Saul had always been a hardworking man. When he graduated high school, he started working in the limestone quarry with his father. He descended into the valleys every day for almost forty years, carrying a mallet and chisel, to split blocks of sediment hauled from the ground, crushing them to dust.

On his last day, the foreman came and shook Saul's hand. "It's been good having you aboard," he said. Saul stared down into the valley and watched the drills eviscerate the walls of terrain, slowly chipping away, piece by piece, turning solid earth into canyon. He reached out and shook the foreman's hand, wiped the white powder from his face, and headed to the bar. He sat sipping a cold beer, still wearing his tool belt, and thought about his early retirement. He hadn't asked to leave early and wasn't even interested in the pension. But the job had recently purchased new motherboards for the power drills, and he couldn't remember how to operate them.

"Please," he pleaded with the foreman. "If we get the old motherboards back, I can do this job."

The foreman shook his head, not looking Saul in the eyes. "It's time," he said. "Nobody has to know why."

"It's just my short term," Saul said, tapping his temple with a finger. "I need more time with the manuals."

The foreman rested a hand on Saul's shoulder. "I'm sorry, Saul," he said.

Saul had been good at his job, reliable, strong. He always took pride in the work, until now, when he sat at the bar and thought about how he hadn't done much with his life except spend his days hollowing out the earth.

In the waiting room, the blonde nurse had reappeared sometime before and sat down next to him. "Mr. Huber," she said, resting a manicured hand on his knee. "I know it's hard." He shifted away from her. "Mr. Huber," she repeated. "If you want to say goodbye to your wife, now's the time."

"This has happened before," he said, "but she was always okay." He fixed his eyes on the fish in the corner aquarium. He could see the nurse nod in the reflection of the glass.

"We'll be moving her soon," she said.

"She said she wasn't going anywhere," Saul said. He wondered if there were tubes in her throat. He wondered if she already had a tag on her toe. He knew it wasn't fair for Emily to see her like that. As her father, he should make the death manageable for her. She needed his protection. He didn't take his eyes away from the fish cutting streaks through the water in the tank. "Is she covered?" he asked. "I don't want to see her under a sheet."

"She's in her bed," the nurse said. "She looks peaceful." She stood and reached out a hand to Saul. "Shall we go together?"

Saul watched as a turtle in the aquarium swam to the surface and gulped for air. Then he nodded and reached for the nurse's outstretched hand.

Seeing her in that bed, memories knotted in Saul's throat. They all came rushing at once, messy as a finger painting, all the colors running together. There were so many Saul felt like he couldn't wade through them. Couldn't choose just one to focus on. It was like the drone of a power drill in his brain, hammering so loudly he couldn't hear the words being spoken to him, couldn't open his eyes in the bright fluorescent lights. Everything, it seemed, was lost in a buzz of noise.

The nurse waited for a moment in the room, standing just near enough to Saul that he could smell her perfume. Different from the scent Henrietta wore. Henrietta always smelled like lilacs. But then Saul wasn't sure if it was lilacs or roses or lilies or those pink flowers that grew in bright fluffy balls, climbing their way up the trellis in their garden. He couldn't remember what those flowers were called. Couldn't remember what they smelled like. He turned to Henrietta for help; she always remembered the names of things for him. His knees went weak. "I need to sit down," he said. "Her purse. Get me her purse."

The nurse left the room and came back with a giant Ziploc bag that held Henrietta's things. Her purse. Her gloves. Her car keys. He unzipped the leather purse and fished around until he found a small bottle of perfume. *Gardenia*, the label read. His heart snared. He hadn't even been close. He found a pen and wrote the word carefully, in block letters on the handkerchief he kept in his pocket, then sprayed two squirts of the perfume into the fabric and brought it to his nose. When he looked up, the nurse was gone. He hadn't seen her slip back into the hallway but was grateful she'd left him alone.

Henrietta wasn't wearing any makeup. She never left the house without putting her face on, and Saul knew she would be embarrassed to be seen this way. He found a bottle of foundation in her purse and patted it under her eyes where dark circles had formed. He had watched her perform the same application every morning for the past thirty-nine years. Even now, if he closed his eyes, he could imagine each step. He could remember the way her fingers traced the lines in her face, remember the angle at which she held a tube of lipstick. He picked up a circular puff next. He knew it was important but couldn't remember what it was for. He had seen it every morning. His breath raced. He squeezed his eyes shut, trying to force the memory to the surface. "I'm so sorry, Henny," he said. And then it came like a shot of lightning. An image. He remembered the time Emily got into her mother's makeup and powdered her entire face. To Saul, she looked like the workers he used to see coming out of the limestone quarries. Pallid. Ghostly. My Emily, he thought. He should call her to break the news.

Henrietta was wearing just a white cotton slip as a nightgown. When she was living, Saul saw every breath rise and fall through the thin layer of cotton, but now it clung to her body, painfully still. He thought if he stared at it long enough, he might see her chest rise, catch that brief moment of hope before it slipped gracefully from her lungs. He leaned close, imagining he could still hear the steady rhythm of her heartbeat. He watched the frozen fabric intently until suddenly, in a jolt of hot air, the fabric fell. A breath. Saul reeled back, not letting his eyes leave her chest, willing the slip to rise again, for Henrietta to cough back to life. He watched, eyes wide, helpless, but the fabric did not move.

When Emily arrived, Saul was tucking the blankets under Henrietta's mattress. He looked up and felt his breath catch in his throat. "H-Henny?" he said.

"Oh, Daddy," Emily said. Even in adulthood, she hadn't outgrown this endearment. Her eyes were red, her face wet. She wrapped her arms around Saul's neck and cried into his shoulder, like she had done as a child. Of course, Saul thought, stroking his daughter's hair. My Emily.

After a moment, she sat delicately at the edge of the bed, reached for her mother's yellowed hand, and pressed her mother's fingers against her lips. Some of her black mascara had dripped onto Henrietta's hand. Saul wanted to wipe the blackness off with his hanky, but didn't want to rub away the scent of Henrietta's perfume. "You can come and stay with me awhile," he said. "You'll need some time."

Emily nodded. She wiped the wetness from her eyes and sighed. "I can't believe she's gone." Her voice tightened. She covered her face with her hands.

Saul shifted in his chair. He wanted to reach out and rest a hand on his daughter's shoulder. He wanted to pull her on his lap and tell her it would be fine, like he had done when she was a little girl. "I'll call someone to bring your bed out of storage," he said. "They can set it up in your old room."

Emily shook her head, her face still covered. Her voice came out muffled from between her palms. "I just can't believe she's gone."

"We can hang the pink canopy again. Keep you safe from the nightmares."

Emily looked up at him. "What?"

"Your magical canopy," Saul said. "The one we hung to keep the monsters out."

"Daddy, what you're talking about," Emily said. "I never had a canopy."

"Of course you did," he said. "Your friend Bonnie Campbell from next door was so jealous." He tried to smile. "You remember, don't you?"

Emily's mouth hung open. She shook her head. "Daddy, who's Bonnie Campbell?" Her face had lost its color.

Sweat trickled down Saul's neck. His heart pounded. He pulled the handkerchief from his pocket and wiped it across his forehead. The sudden smell of Henrietta blinded him. He staggered. "What?" he said. "What did you say?"

His mind raced. He saw everything, felt it all at once, in one messy puddle of gardenia and power drills and neon fish and flashing sirens. The limestone crushed to powder. The sheets fluttered. His body slid down the plastic seat. He heard Emily crying from the other side of a canyon. He knew it was her, but he couldn't find her. Couldn't reach out a hand to comfort her as she shouted, frantic, for a nurse.

In the days following the funeral, Saul was grateful to Emily for helping him pack up the house. "It's okay, Daddy," she said, but she didn't look him in the eyes. She reached for a vase on the kitchen counter. "Keep, sell, or donate?" she said.

Saul stared at the vase in her hand. It was porcelain with blue flowers. It looked cheap. "I don't know," he said.

Emily set the vase in a box. "Donate then," she said. She picked up a wooden cutting board. "Keep, sell, or donate?" Her voice shook.

Saul picked up a pile of yellowed newspapers and dumped them into a trash bin. He heard Emily exhale. She dropped the cutting board into a box, then fished out the newspapers. "These are for wrapping glasses," she said. "Can you focus, Daddy? Please?"

For the next few minutes, Emily worked in silence, dropping things into random boxes. It hurt Saul to see her so angry.

"I just got confused," he said.

Emily looked up. "What did you do," she asked. "What are you talking about?"

"Bonnie Campbell," he said. "She was my sister's friend. I just got confused."

Emily cleared her throat. "You told me that already," she said. She turned her back and started rooting through the cupboards. "What about these," she said. "Keep, sell, or donate?"

He couldn't see what she was holding. It didn't matter. "Just leave it," he said. "I'll finish this later."

"You're coming home with me," Emily said. "We discussed this. Remember?"

"I'm not a child," he snapped.

Emily rested the fingers of one hand on her forehead. She breathed in deeply through her nose.

"I'll finish this," he said.

Emily nodded. "Fine," she said. "I'll just be in the other room."

When she was gone, Saul eased himself onto the floor next to the boxes. He sifted through the few sheets of paper and photographs Emily decided he should keep. One crystal bell. A blanket. A sterling silver spoon. He picked the items up one by one and held them in his hands. He felt the curve of the bell with his fingers, the weight of the silver in his palm, but these items held no meaning. He couldn't remember them.

And yet he didn't want to return them to the box. Beside him sat a green notebook and he flipped through its pages. He recognized his handwriting. *Baby Blanket for Emily*, one note said. He picked up the half-knitted blanket and ran his fingers over the stitches. That's right, he thought. I remember. He wanted to place the blanket in the box marked *Keep*, as if that meant he could hold onto it forever, but he was too afraid to let it leave his hands. He closed his eyes and could hear the click of Henrietta's needles. When he brought the blanket to his nose, he could almost smell the gardenia.

Adele Ne Jame

Two Poems

A Deadly Embrace

Two men fighting fell together into the sea and drowned.
Their bodies were found washed up on the shore,
lifeless but still locked in a deadly embrace.
—from an account of battles between Druzes
and Christians by Iskandar Abkariyus (1826–1885)

1

You see heaven above a hillside and more
abandoned homes, one after another,
some with doors blown wide open—

others padlocked in this beautiful
mountain village high above the Mediterranean,
here where my parents and their parents

started out, wine makers and goat herders,
with their olive presses and daily sacraments.
As we drive the high road,

my cousin assures us civil peace
is a red line now. When he talks of the war,
his Arabic clear, his voice broken,

he says how it reached the Chouf
one September morning
after the Israelis' withdrew having

armed both sides of the sectarian divide
and firing star shells into the sky,
incendiary birds flaring—

the signal—and how for five hours
after that, the slaughter never stopped,
villagers executed in their doorways,

children herded into the fields.
White linen and jasmine.
Two birds in a tree.

This by our neighbors, he says,
and between one breath and another:
We had even attended each other's weddings.

2

Still, my cousins love the village,
Yalla, come back, they say
it's paradise on earth—

your ancestral home.
The heart sings the same songs.
You may love Lebanon,

but it doesn't love you back
my father might have said after
it showed us Death on this mountain.

3

Later we walk the village streets together,
climb to a stony courtyard,
You see falling pine branches

and racing red clouds—
the view is splendid, splendid—
the peak of Mount Lebanon

laced with snow and cedars,
an extravagant pewter sky,
and in the cool wind,

the mulberry flourishing.
Let's go my cousin says under his breath
after we have transgressed the desolate

privacy of someone's shamble of
a home—beds of goat's hair
stuffed into ticking on metal frames,

wads of it in a tumble on the floor
below tall arching windows open
to the huge world. Like a shade you walk

through the courtyard again—
it is littered with broken glass and cups.
This is where a woman boiled coffee

for her neighbors in the afternoon light
as you see it now—awash with copper
falling over the terraced valley.

To one side a rusted iron drum,
the bold letters on it stamped SYRIA,
collects pure rainwater for no one.

4

Early the next morning, we sit together,
inhale lavender under an arbor of vines,
beds of chamomile around us in the chill.

We drink strong coffee,
tuck spiced olives and lebne into Syrian bread—
our breakfast under the mountain sun.

Then we walk to St. Michel's
to hear the divine liturgy, they say,
transported from Antioch

and sung in Greek and Arabic.
Inside, crystal chandelier light falls
on the images of saints whose suffering

is transformed into transcendence—
you see this in the eyes—
There along the wall, to honor the dead,

the names of sixty-three souls inscribed,
those set aflame in the earth here,
and among them your own.

The oldest village woman gently pulls you aside
and whispers *the Druze houses on the mountain slope
above us are situated there for good aim.*

She gestures rapid gunfire—
the sound of bullets. You think racing
red clouds and jasmine, a deadly embrace.

Then, all at once, as if over deep water
the music begins, a choir of voices resounding
has us falling to our knees in prayer—

the liturgy is gorgeously sung in undulating
Arabic phrasing—on this mountain
in this country—it's as if the angels

were weeping in the crashing wind for
all the beautiful bodies of the drowned—
those in sea water, those not.

Then you reel from the tremor—
the pounding of your temporal arteries on fire,
from every cell of the heart's loud cry—

here in this monastery, this cold morning,
you know more than ever
we are all diving for air at the door of God.

Grief, A Revolving Landscape

1

Dreaming in Arabic, flying red clouds
hang over the high Chouf village.
A young boy dresses early by lamp light,

does his morning chores in the cold sun.
Leaning heavily into the cedar wind,
he lugs fire wood into the kitchen

to keep the heat going. In this dream
his parents live, his sisters
have long, dark hair they sweep up

into heavy braids. Julia, the young one,
wears olive wood beads and carries
buckets of rainwater to the garden

while their mother steams milk with
cardamom and sugar for them.
In this dream they live to grow up,

marry, even have children of their own.
In this dream, the boy is not yet a grief
stricken survivor of war. Village gunfire

has not done its work, the blades of
his neighbors knives have not
slashed the throats of their goats

in the fields or those still sleeping
in their beds. He does not hear
their stiffening cries.

The house is not yet stone vacant
and the front gates are not yet chained up
and rusting in the rain.

2

What does this have to do with us,
with me—as I climb that mountain,
in the March snow far into the future,

see those terraced gardens that will bloom
half a world away under the shinning red clouds?
Our questions are locked up in those walls,

in that village, but not so amorphous
grief. It keeps moving—
like pollutants carried by ocean currents that

fill estuaries and seep into ground water.
Our bodies mark it in a hundred ways—
the sirocco storm of it, the empty boat of it.

There is the beaten-down slouch of the shoulders,
the wheels of our own night terrors
like blue smoke. Under the microscope

the landscape of our weeping,
our dried human tears, mostly crystallized
salt in extreme detail, they tell us,

a landscape different from all other tears,
different from ones shed in joy or fear;
our emotional terrain cataloged—

more than that: the sum of our collective
human experience, they say,
and dried there too, enkephalins,

the body's narcotic, a natural
pain killer, a moment of sweet rescue.
If only we could live on it—

or rest at will—the way
a cat blinks away the world when
it dozes on a windowsill in the sun.

3

Years after the boy's exile, another life of
absolute silence
spent in that holy city of grief where

you know you will lose everything,
I say, finally, I lived there with you, father,
saw the daily labor of your mourning,

carried it with me into the future
and back to the huge Beirut air—
It rose up from me like a cloud of fog

and settled heavy again when I found
your vacant village home,
climbed the rusted gate to the terraced

gardens you tended, and where,
suddenly, I saw an almond tree sure to
blossom again into darkness

and where the red poppies, in the wind
you loved and already budding,
had broken through a drift of blinding snow.

Connie Pan

The Patron Saint of Exits

The first time I saw Elsa, she was twirling a key ring around her finger. The keys sounded like bells. Not a soft jingling in the ear canals but the dull clanking of metal. Church bells. Maybe a B flat. For a moment, time paused—the sunshine mixed with her hair, accenting the reds and oranges light and saltwater made possible—but the bells kept ringing. When she walked through the door, she walked right into my life. At the time, I was just Pancho's invisible roommate. Elsa never asked for my acceptance, but she was welcome from that moment. Such an aimless spirit. She haunted me then, and she haunts me now because she is no longer here.

We lived on a sleepy, stony island in Hawai'i, a proud and sunny archipelago. Most think island life is no worries, but island life is more than working your shift, clocking out, cat napping and surfing. Not to say the place isn't full of beauty, but most of the time beauty ends in heartbreak. I know that as much as anyone. Thousands of miles from any continental coast, each island turns in on itself. This isolation forces a small world. Everybody knows everyone. I'm not talking about names. Not only do we know the names of each other, we know your first and second cousins. We know how to draw the line from them to you. We know where you live, which means we know where your grandparents live too. We know where you went to school, elementary, intermediate and high school, and we know who you run with. We know your business.

A local, Elsa's dad left the islands when he joined the military. He probably wanted to see the world. He met a haole lady on the Mainland. They had a baby and married. Not entirely sure of the order. The math cuts it close. He returned when Elsa was ten. She was a smart girl, an honor roll student, well-mannered, a little shy. She hid a few steps behind her father and mother, barely visible around his tree-trunk legs and her huge purse. They moved in with his mom and dad up Lahainaluna. His parents own a popular ma and pa shop, Noodles Now. Every summer Elsa waitressed there. She bustled up and down the bar-style seating with steaming piles of chow fun, saimin and pancit lined up her right arm. Her dad sent her to the same small private school he attended, and after eighth-grade graduation, he sent her to the same public high school where he once was a handsome shortstop.

The summer between Elsa's switch from private to public school, her parents separated. Everyone could tell it was against the father's will. Whenever anyone brought it up, he looked sad, privately mourning the life that was no longer his. Most of the reasons that flittered around were gossip, dalliances dreamed up between neighbors and classmates over shopping carts while passing each other in the produce section.

"I heard his wife when cheat with her coworker," said an old classmate, knotting a bag of garlic bulbs.

"You think? I thought the father was too rough on the daughter. Strict the family," countered a neighbor, searching for immaculate tomatoes.

"Either way, that girl's a saint," the other said, thinning her lips.

Elsa wasn't coping well. The divorce tore her up. She began hanging with upperclassmen. We called the kids they ran around with vagrants because they called themselves that. Expatriates cursing their homes. You could find them at the beach at night, their cases of cheap beer, Milwaukee's Best and Red Dog, hidden in the sand. The cheapest way of keeping it cold was a quick way of concealing it. If someone came to check on the vagrants, they kicked sand over the cans and pretended they were just talking and spacing at the ocean. Most nights, they huddled around the beer, crowded onto pink and sea-foam green lawn chairs. On nights when the hotel security guards were being bitches, you could hear their squawking echo through the kiawe trees. They didn't own cars. They littered the highway with their thumbs out. They had a crystal-meth chic about them. They earned the holes in their denim by sitting on their asses or crawling on their knees. The holes made it easier to inspect if their legs were turning blue. They wore faded, oversized t-shirts. Band t-shirts. T-shirts with phrases like "Dank of Hawaii." T-shirts with holes in the seams. Girls wore boys' t-shirts, and boys wore girls' t-shirts. Everyone wore anybody's t-shirt. I guess the only prerequisite was that you had to pick it up off the floor. The girls donned three-day-old makeup. The boys depended on the ocean for baths. Some of this I knew, some things Elsa told me when we knew each other, some things I intuited, and some things I understood later.

I was nineteen. I didn't graduate high school. My roommate was a drug dealer nicknamed Pancho. We lived in a small two-bedroom house in an OK neighborhood, where most of the other houses bore multigenerational families. The houses were so crowded, families set up their living rooms and put extra refrigerators on their lanais. At the tables, kids did homework; adults played poker; families ate boiled peanuts, mochi crunch and shrimp chips while watching TV. In the extra ice boxes, they stocked beer in green bottles: Heineken, Steinlager, Moosehead. They stocked cans of Coors Light. They stocked soda, POG and bottled water. They froze fresh fish they caught, fish dropped off by family who had a good day on the water, fish bought on the side of the road from locals who arranged tents, chairs, coolers and signs that lured, AHI FOR SALE, before the sun got too hot. Watching my neighbors on their lanais, I was jealous. I spent most of my time in my bedroom or at work. There were no couches or refrigerators on our porch. We had rules.

Pancho slung meth or whatever was cool that week. I was a line cook at the Kahana Bar and Grill, where I met Pancho, a dishwasher. We sat on empty kegs on the back dock between lunch and dinner rushes. We exchanged our stories while hurling trash bags into the dumpster. Always looking for a way to get ahead, he made better money dealing, so he switched to part-time dishwashing for full-time pushing. Since I was the only one he trusted, he asked me to move in. I was his alibi with my legit job to help pay the rent, electric, trash and water, but I didn't actually pay bills. Because Pancho was using me, I got to live for free. It was his way of compensating me for being his vein of legality. Pancho didn't like to owe anyone anything. And as for me, I had nowhere else to go and nothing to lose. But I'd soon discover nothing was free.

Pancho's customers came and went during business hours. His traffic was only allowed to frequent between nine and five. He figured those were honorable hours, the hours of the yuppie. Usually nighttime traffic is tagged with deviance: paramours, handcuffs, uppers. The FBI was coming down hard on small-time dealers to get them to snitch on their bosses, and he didn't want to land a surveillance van on the end of our street. Traffic that didn't leave the house before five had to stay. After five, we didn't answer the door, and we didn't answer the phone.

Pancho called the shots. He was the mean dictator of our almost invisible drug world. He was becoming someone I didn't recognize. I missed the Pancho who gushed about going somewhere, his head in the palms, bumping on coconuts. His eyes used to be bright with dreams; now Pancho didn't even sleep. His late nights dug graves beneath his eyes. The change in his personality formed a rift between us and I didn't know how to tell this strange drug-lord how I felt, so I tiptoed around him. I was terrified of how he would react, what he would say. I was scared of what kind of hold he had on me.

Elsa came and went between Pancho's hours. She didn't have the desperation of a user. Always accompanying a friend, she never arrived alone. The drugs seemed like a party favor to her, a hat she wore for the occasion that she thought ugly or ridiculous or not her style elsewhere. She never mentioned boyfriends, girlfriends, family or a home. Most of the people who bought from Pancho talked a lot. Mainly because they were on some amphetamine or another. She only talked when talked to or when someone asked her a question because she wasn't rude—just quiet.

Elsa sat and tugged at her sleeves with her right leg tucked under her.

She had a complexion hard to pinpoint: lighter than her father, darker than her mother. A pretty hapa haole with obsidian hair, a golden tan and slender bones, dainty wrists and ankles like brittle twigs. She hugged herself like she was her only friend, which made me think she wanted to disappear.

I sat bewildered in her ghostly aura. Wordless. Nothing falling off my tongue. A furrowed brow. Lonesome. She was an enigma. At that point, everything I knew about her I had learned through Pancho's customers, from the answers to their questions.

"Do you have a boyfriend?"

No.

"Do you have a girlfriend?"

No.

"Are you a lesbian?"

No.

"Are you Native American?"

No.

"Are you Brazilian?"

No.

"Are you Portuguese?"

No.

"A gypsy?"

No, the light of my dreams said, sliding a jade pendant along her gold chain. And *gypsy* is considered a derogatory term. They prefer to be called the Roma people. They travel in groups and find work, set up camp, build fires and move on whenever they feel like it. They're looked down upon because they don't share middle-class values, so people think they're witches.

This was the most I had ever heard her say, and it made me fall a little more in love with her because I got her. The only reason why they were looked down on is because they preferred living on the fringes. Society wanted them to work real jobs, buy a house and drop roots just like them. I think Elsa liked the idea of being a gypsy. It was the first time her smile pierced me, and it made me smile because she was kind of like a gypsy and I was kind of like society. I wanted her to stay put, right there, on my cranberry couch. While gypsies carried suitcases, Elsa carried a purse. I glimpsed inside it. She fidgeted with it often. I saw tampons, animal crackers, an extra t-shirt. Panties. Toothpaste. A magazine.

"Do you go to school?"

Sometimes.

"How old are you?"

Fifteen.

"Do you have any brothers or sisters?"

No.

But even the facts appeared blurry. I would have continued to find Elsa mysterious even if I pinned her down and spread her out between glass like a pressed butterfly and labeled all her parts. While gypsies traveled in caravans, even sitting in a group, Elsa seemed completely alone. She never left with anyone. She never waited for anyone. She loomed asexual and disinterested.

Every night before I fell asleep, I thought of her. I meditated on her face, her sad eyes, because I remembered something my mother told me when I was little—I suffered nightmares—"whatever you think about before you go to bed will be the content of your dreams." It didn't always work, but on the mornings it hadn't, I woke up wishing with my fingers crossed.

It was a Thursday night, and it was after five. Everyone was tweaking. I was just drinking beer. Pancho stood. He turned on the TV to an old UFC fight. He shadowboxed to the door, throwing combos and ducking invisible punches. He locked the screen door. Closed the front door. Turned the lock on the door knob. Pulled the chain through and twisted the dead bolt.

What I hated most about five were the jonesers who lurked around hoping for a free line from Pancho's stash. Pancho called those party favors. He left them crushed up in a neat line on his toilet seat. The bastard did it because it was degrading, and an addict could never resist a freebie.

The only way to snort it was on your knees, your head bent, your neck bare. His party favors boosted business because it left his customers wanting. That was one of the many reasons I didn't use. I didn't want to owe anyone anything either.

I knew Elsa had lost track of time because she scanned the walls and scrambled through her purse when Pancho locked down the house. She knew the rules, that there was nothing she could do. She eyeballed her forced company: a fake platinum blonde with an inch of mousy brown roots wearing a red sequined tube-top that intended to look sexy, a mid-twentyish guy with a beanie jerked so far down on his forehead you could barely see his eyes, and Elsa's friend, Karina. She fucked Pancho for drugs. Elsa bit her bottom lip.

"Would you like a beer?" Those were the first words I spoke to her.

Sure. That was the first word she spoke to me.

You think you know your neighbors, but you never know what is happening next door, within their walls, after the doors close. I fantasized about their lives. I liked to think it resembled their time spent on lanais. *Were they happy?* I imagined them eating dinner at cramped tables with placemats. Their dinners didn't need cloth napkins, festive napkin holders, or salad and entrée forks, just a steady flow of conversation where the parents inquired about their children's grades, friends and thoughts. If my neighbors' minds wandered as much as mine, I hoped they were wrong about us.

I didn't want to be an outlaw. I didn't want to be guilty by association. Usually, I didn't even want to know what happened in our house. Usually, I escaped to my room, shut the door and stretched out on my single bed. Living there was an out-of-body experience. I focused on things like my bimonthly paycheck. Each week got me further and further away from Pancho. That fall, I only stuck around because of Elsa. Because I was dormant—somewhere between life and death—and she made me feel alive.

Elsa sat, hiding behind a curtain of dark hair, wavy like limu. I searched for her face while mousy roots and Karina tried to up-sex each other for free shit. Pancho took them into his room. Sequins emerged wiping her mouth and readjusting. Karina followed deflated. Guy in the beanie slouched there, probably wishing he had tits, because he had already spent his last ten dollars.

Elsa rose and tiptoed, groping in the dark. She found the hallway, and from the sound of a door locking, she found the bathroom. Finally I could breathe regularly and, because Elsa was gone, found myself observing other things. On the TV screen, a man in red shorts bound a smaller man in a leg lock. His body curled above him, a wave, threatening him with his power. He punched him over and over again. On the temple, on the ear, the jaw. Blood splattered the mat. There you could examine shadows from other beatings. They resembled Rorschach inkblot test images: winged creatures, a butterfly conservatory on the floor, a sky of nimbus clouds holding rain. Pancho broke the repetitive slapping sounds by saying, "Rodriguez is a pussy." He flipped down bottle blonde's tube-top and jiggled a full breast in his hand. Creeper eyed the areola. It was the size of a breakfast sausage patty. I looked away quickly, not wanting to have anything in common with Creeper or Pancho. I refused to bond over the naked parts of tube-top girl. Karina shifted awkwardly in the dark. The couch's wood beams moaned. The sound bought a look of query. Otherwise, she had been forgotten.

Disturbed by my company, I checked on Elsa. A slit of light seeped out from underneath the crack of the bathroom door. I tapped lightly.

"You all right?"

Yeah.

"Do you need anything?"

No.

"You've been in there a while."

I know.

"Call if you change your mind." I turned to walk down the hallway to fetch another beer. I made it a couple steps before she stopped me.

Don't go, she said.

I pivoted. The shadows of her feet lingered in the crack of light. Had there not been a door there, we would have stood face to face.

Do you ever feel like you don't belong? She turned. I heard her back against the door as she slid down to sit on the floor.

I mimicked her. "All the time."

I hate it here, but I can't stand home either.

"Why? What's at home?" She was silent except for the tiny sounds her twitching made. I guessed the words she wanted to say weren't easy. I waited.

I don't know why I'm telling you this, but my mom's a drunk. She was quiet. Probably sampling the way the words tasted in her mouth. *Did they leave her palate sour? Did she wish for them to soar back in and remain a secret?* It felt good saying that, she said, and exhaled.

The electricity in the air changed. It vibrated at a lower frequency. "If you want, my room is right across the hall. You can't leave, but you can stay in there. I'll sleep on the couch," I said. My genuine concern for Elsa's well-being mixed with desperation. She pondered it for minutes, and the minutes passed slowly. I could feel the warmth through the door from my back and her back pressing against the same spot. Our breathing synchronized, like how two people walking together fall into step naturally. I heard shuffling. She opened the door, and we faced each other. She looked as if she had been crying. Her eyes were red. She held her purse like a shield. It hid her torso. She smelled like moonflowers.

Thank you. That guy in the beanie creeps me out.

I laughed and opened my door for her.

She smiled a sheepish, one-sided grin.

I walked back to the living room and sunk into Elsa's spot on the couch.

In the morning she was gone. Everything in its place: the bed untouched, the pillows fluffed, the comforter slack equal on both sides, the top of the sheet and blanket folded down. It was as if the women from the Children's House of Hope, armed with their bed-making drills, had coached Elsa. Other than the faint smell of moonflowers, it was as if she had never been there.

A night passed. Another night passed. And another night passed. Elsa called late Sunday night.

I knew something was wrong. The phone rang and rang and rang, which wasn't unusual. What was unusual was that I answered. Pancho glared at me and raised his left hand to say, No, don't, or to indicate five. We don't answer the phone after five. She was crying. It was the kind of sobbing that grabbed you by your floating ribs and shook you.

Hi, it's me.

"Hey," I could barely hear her. She was whispering. Punk music blared in the background. I imagined her hand cupping the air around her lips and the mouthpiece. She was telling me another secret.

Can you pick me up?

"What happened?"

My mom was pissed I didn't come home the other night. She called me a whore and poured her drink on me, so I hit her. She hit me back. Elsa tried to catch her breath between words and whimpers. She barricaded my door. She said she's sending me away.

"If she barricaded the door, how can I pick you up?"

Wait outside my window.

I dropped the receiver in the cradle and looked up to find Pancho scowling at me.

"What the fuck?" Pancho spat.

"It was Elsa. She needs my help."

"I don't give a shit who the fuck it was. She's no different than any other bitch."

"She's not a bitch, Pancho."

"Oh," he said, nodding, just beginning to understand. "So, you like this Elsssa." The way he said her name made my ears burn. "What the fuck do you think is going to come of that? She's a druggie."

I felt nothing but hate for him. "You don't know what you're talking about. You don't know her."

"And you think you do? You're broken, and you found someone just as broken as you to cling to. You think because you talked to her for two seconds there's something there?"

"I don't need this."

"Don't walk away from me. We're not done. You need to hear this. You broke the rules!"

"Fuck the rules! Fuck you! You think you're so much better than everyone. You're blind. You're going nowhere, Pancho. Wait," I turned on my heel to look him in the eye while I said, "you have a good chance of going to jail." I stomped to the front door, untwisted the dead bolt. Pulled the chain through. Let it drop. Turned the lock on the doorknob. Flung the door open. Unlocked the screen door, slammed it into the wood and yelled into the street, "Oh my God, it's after five. Don't answer the phone! Don't leave the house!"

On the sidewalk, a lady in running shorts, power walking her golden retriever, jumped at the sound of me. She held her fists high, next to her chest. Her brown ponytail bounced. She pumped her arms fast. The leash between her and the dog danced. She turned, eyeing me like I was crazy before crossing the street to forge more space between us. It looked safer over there. No one screamed into the street. No one had a livid Pancho invading their space, breathing down their neck, trying to intimidate.

"You're crazy," Pancho said.

"No, Pancho. You're the one that's fucking crazy." I left the door wide open, wide open for the outside to glimpse Pancho's world. While I stomped across the lawn to my truck, I kicked everything I came in contact with. Newspapers. An empty garbage can. The mailbox.

When I looked in the rearview mirror I wished for an explosion, a smoking pyre, sirens. I wanted it to look like sloppy shambles. The remains after a hurricane pounded through. There was hardly a path of destruction. The mailbox stood erect with a closed door, the trash can upright. The papers were intact, just in different places than before. The orange plastic bags and twist ties had done their job, but the line from Pancho to me was severed beyond repair. He retreated.

I knew exactly what he would do. He would close the screen door and lock it. Close the front door. Turn the lock on the door knob. Pull the chain through and twist the dead bolt, locking all his dark inside.

Outside Elsa's window, birds of paradise adorned the bushes like vibrant ornaments. The exotic orange and blue blooms looked like a family of cranes frozen in extravagant poses, their backs arched and necks bent. Waterfowl in flight. I gazed up towards Elsa's lit room, appreciating the brightness of the stars and the way the clouds looked like cotton balls stretched as thin as spider webs. It looked like I could reach up and put my hand through them. The stars pulsated and swirled and pumped like my heart.

She came to the window, waved and punched the screen. It bent, and she pulled it inside. She stuck her head out. I thought of Rapunzel. I had many romanticized images of how we would fall in love. It wasn't supposed to happen like that, but I'd take anything she gave me. First she threw down her purse. Then she hoisted her body onto the windowsill and jumped. I reached out my arms, like a child begging for a hug, and waited for velocity—hoping we could vanish.

Pat Matsueda

My Friend Looks
at the Horizon

Sitting with Tom at
Hau Tree Lanai, we reach
that point in a conversation where

understanding brings silence

we've been talking about the Aikaus:
Gerald, who hung himself
after stabbing his seven-year-old boy;
Eddie, who sought help for his shipmates
then was lost at sea

And I am reminded of Mahealani:
killed by her husband and then hung;
the two found side by side

Tom looks at the horizon,
beyond the mothers, children, and lovers
who claim the shore with affection

Noticing the blue perfection between
ocean and sky, he tells me of
a future swim to Molokaʻi,

no fanfare, no escort; his last wishes
will already be known to his wife

The swim is thirty miles long from where we sit
under the trees on this June morning,
and when he tells me of his plan, his eyes
are as placid as the sea

Friends who meet twice yearly to talk
of many things,
then the last important one:

not leaving it up to fate but choosing the way to die—

the way we might pull our bodies out of the sea

Angela Nishimoto

Start with Mustard

Young men sharp as mustard,
the tang of the spice on your tongue
searing, tears streak.

Young men green as wasabi,
the freshening causing your nose to run.
You sip green tea to cease the flow.

Young men snappy as ginger,
warm—sweet, even, underground
rhizome. Almost a root.

Young men hot as chili,
sweat beading your brow,
rolling down the sides of your face
as you dare to take one more bite.

Lillian Howan

The Blue Medium

I t is my profession to be lost. When I was an apprentice, my teacher took me to a grove of mape trees, a place where sunlight was hidden, disappearing into the canopy of leaves. The wood of the mape was dark, nearly black, and the trunks opened like wings. "Losing your way is easy," said my teacher.

We had left his pick-up truck by the side of the road and were wandering through the elephant-ear taro that grew in the shadows beneath the mape trees. There arose the scent of things unseen: the earth damp below the thickness of leaves, the smoke from garbage burning far away. Over the ground, the mape spread its roots in serpentine ridges.

The teacher walked to where two roots ran close together, the gap within curving like a narrow boat. "Sit here," he said, and I shook out an empty rice sack and placed it inside. A cloud of mosquitos rose from the ground as I sat. "Are there spirits here?" I asked.

"Sit down and don't move," said the teacher. He was the age of my grandfather and smelled of camphor oil and Hundred Flowers liniment.

I looked up above at the web of branches, the green darkness that obscured the sky. "Will spirits come if I wait?"

"I'll return in the morning," said the teacher walking away towards the road.

I crossed my legs and waited. The air was hot and breathless with the odor of decaying leaves. Mosquitos whined around my ears, and I heard the ocean in the distance, the sound of the waves breaking and receding, the breath of the ocean inhaled and exhaled and inhaled again.

Every day of my apprenticeship, I had sat, motionless for hours inside the teacher's house or outside in his garden of mango trees and tilapia fish ponds. "Look here," said the teacher, pointing to the crack between his doors, double doors, the bottom corner of one broken and partially eaten by termites. "No—you're looking at this side, look here at the center between the doors. Not more to one side or to the other." On the other side of the doors, someone was brooming, sweeping the leaves fallen during the night. "Breathe slowly. Don't be distracted looking this way and that."

I learned to remain still. I learned to focus on the line where the double doors met. I learned to be silent.

"Listen," the teacher always said.

"What am I listening for?" I asked.

"Listen here"—he thumped the center of my chest. "You're just listening with your ears. And what good are those? You won't hear anything." He bent slowly down, and lifting my toes, he pointed at the soles of my feet. "Here is where you listen."

The teacher heard the voices of the spirit world. He would sit in a room other than the one where I sat, the house silent with only the *vini vini* birds chattering in the trees outside. Nothing would be spoken, and then I would hear him beginning to sing. His song was different from the songs I heard everyday, the *san ko*, the mountain songs of my great-grandmother or the love songs my aunts sang as they folded the wash. The teacher's song was tuneless, without pattern like an endless thread, his voice twisting, rising, and then disappearing.

When I first started as an apprentice, I was a small boy and I asked the teacher many questions. What did they say? What did they look like? My questions were constant, but the teacher's answer was always the same: listen, be still, listen.

My uncle Freddy, who was only one year older and like a brother, goaded me at home with gruesome tales of *tupapaus*, the spirits of the dead. "They'll catch you and eat you alive," he said. He told me that a boy in Bora Bora had been captured by a sorcerer and many days later part of his head was found under his family's doorstep. "Crabs were crawling out of his skull," said Freddy, "and his eyes were eaten away."

I recounted this to the teacher and he laughed. "Is it true?" I asked.

"Maybe you should go home and not return anymore," he replied still laughing.

"Is it true?"

"Go sit by the doors," he said. "Maybe a ghost will appear and explain these things to you."

I sat and sat. Every day I listened and the years of my apprenticeship accumulated waiting for the spirit voices to sing for me.

I sat, the hours passing, and the end of the day approached. The branches of the mape curved above and veils of light fell through the leaves when the wind was still. I tried to think of my breath flowing in and out, and then I was thinking about dinner.

The nut of the mape tree was kidney-shaped and enclosed in a wooden shell. Along the road to Papeete, street vendors sold mapes boiled and strung on *niau*, the thin sticks running through the centers of palm leaves. Grandfather sometimes bought mapes, and then the younger cousins danced about, their hands outstretched, shouting "ma-pay! ma-pay!"—the mapes as large as the palm of their hands. The nut always bore a knife-mark, a cut on the corners and along the flesh where the machete blade had split the shell.

I thought of mapes fallen among the leaves waiting to be gathered. The taste was mild and sweet, and I had all night to sit still, waiting for spirits to appear. I had never seen a spirit, but I had eaten mapes and before the evening light faded, I thought my time better spent searching for something I knew I could find.

The earth was wet and sank like a sponge. I walked over tree roots, twisting along the ground, and the empty hulls of mapes. At home my cousins, Freddy, and my aunts, my grandparents, and parents would be eating dinner: bean curd, dried shrimp, peppers stuffed with finely-ground fish, chicken and black mushrooms. I continued walking—perhaps there were mapes fallen in the shade of the next tree, behind a branch, among the roots.

The sunset light dimmed, and the shadows spread quickly. I turned back, the black trunks of the trees looming, suddenly unfamiliar and unrecognizable, a pattern of vines and leaves dissolving into the unbroken shadow of the night. Where had the teacher asked me to sit? Behind this shadowy ridge of roots? Beyond this field of taro? I had found nothing, not a single nut. There was only the soft, sucking mud beneath my feet and darkness all around. The night descended, and I did not know where I was.

The wind rose, erasing the sound of the ocean. A rooster crowed and a dog began barking. The barking seemed far away, muffled by the dense surrounding trees. It would be a long walk to the nearest house, guided by the glimmer of distant sounds.

Above in the treetops, a seabird awakened and called, a rasping, creaking sound. *A piece of skull*, Freddy had said, *the crabs had swallowed the eyes*. I sat down at the foot of a mape, my back against the trunk, and waited. A ghost was detected by its perfume, I had heard—a scent like frangipani. Along the road that passed before the house where my family lived, trees of frangipani bloomed, the flowers pink and yellow, red and the colors of sunset. The scent crept at night through the open windows over our beds where we slept enveloped in mosquito netting.

My grandfather had once seen a ghost. He told me this story often, talking as he closed the locks to his store near the waterfront of Papeete. He had been bicycling from the town where he played mahjong at night. The road had been empty, his dog following behind as he pedaled along the hedges of hibiscus and crotons. As he turned past the flamboyant trees, he saw someone crossing the road, a woman dressed in white. She was wearing a white hat as if it were Sunday morning and she was on her way to church, but it was night and all the churches were closed. Grandfather slowed his pedaling as the woman walked towards the middle of the road, but his dog ran ahead barking. The woman turned, and Grandfather saw that she held a cluster of grapes in her hand, her face hidden beneath her hat.

Grapes did not grow where we lived, on the island of Tahiti; they were imported and they were rare. Grandfather said these grapes were purple, almost red, shining in the moonlight beneath the woman's hand. Even Fwi-lin his dog stopped barking and paused, whining and sniffing the air. Grandfather swung one leg from his bicycle. The woman stretched out her arm dangling the grapes, and for a moment, Grandfather saw her face—the face of a young girl no older than ten or eleven. She was so young, a child in a woman's dress, that Grandfather shouted in surprise, and then she vanished. Fwi-lin barked and snapped at the air, but there was nothing in the road—no girl, no grapes—only Grandfather alone with his bicycle.

I had tasted grapes once when I was fifteen. I had accompanied Grandfather and Father to a dinner at the house of Monsieur Lesage. Grandfather introduced me, his eldest grandson, and there was polite talk about my interest in languages and the possibility of my being sent to the University of Paris. We were Hakka and, according to Father, the Hakka had a gift for languages. He said this whenever we visited the house of someone French. I never paid attention; I always heard this story—my father explaining that in China we were called the guest people and how for a thousand years we had wandered, across China and Southern Asia, among a multitude of dialects and that we learned to translate one object into many names.

Monsieur Lesage sat in a wicker chair beneath a painting of coconut palms, the colors washed in dark green, purple, and yellow light. He owned two freighters, the *Mareva* and the *Moana Nui,* and transported cargo from the South China Sea to Papeete. He said he had lived in Saigon many years ago and there he heard that the Hakka were the most fanatical, the most secretive; they had lost one of the bloodiest civil wars in history and were said to possess a secret so that they did not fear death.

This was nonsense, Father replied. People always told exotic stories, but in the end everyone was afraid of death. When a war was lost, many died regardless of whether they were afraid or not.

"They died or they came to Tahiti," said Grandfather, and he and Monsieur Lesage laughed. They were both large men and everything about them seemed rectangular and solid—their faces, their backs, their hands. Around us the furniture bore a smooth sheen, chairs and shelves covered with a dustless glow.

We ate beef bourguignon and potatoes dauphinoise in the dining room overlooking the sea, the ceiling fans above turning slowly. At the end of dinner, a plate of cheese accompanied by a bowl of fruit was brought to the table. The fruit was not local, but imported by air—apples, grapes, plums and mirabelles. The fruit was refrigerated, a fine layer of condensation already covering the cold skin. I selected an apple and a plum and picked up my knife. The image of my mother appeared briefly, shaking her head no. "Jonathan why two? And such a large plum," she said. "One is enough."

I glanced at Grandfather—he was puffing on a cigar, the tip turning from ash to incandescent as he inhaled. Father was talking heatedly discussing the Assembly elections, his head bent sideways towards Monsieur Lesage. I reached across the table and plucked a small cluster of grapes. I ate the plum, scooping the red flesh with a spoon, and then I ate the grapes, peeling them one by one. The grapes were yellow-green and the seeds were large and tear-shaped. The apple I ate last, slicing it open with a knife, the red vein around the seed-core curved like a heart.

I thought of apples, red grapes, mapes and beef bourguignon, chicken with black mushrooms—all the food I was not eating and the dinner I had missed. The night stretched endlessly, each moment passing, slow as an hour. I closed my eyes, I opened my eyes, the darkness remained unchanged.

When I first became an apprentice, I imagined myself calling forth different spirits every night, my uncle Freddy and my cousins at my mercy. I saw them fetching the sweetest mangos for me and doing all my homework. No longer would I do the usual chores, feeding the chickens and the pigs, awakening early—Freddy was always still asleep—to bring the bread for breakfast in the morning.

My dreams of glory vanished though when I discovered the nature of my apprenticeship. It was monotonous, long, and relentlessly unremarkable. I had been an apprentice for seven years, and I was sixteen—seventeen in November—and what had I learned? Nothing. No magic formulas, no incantations. No spirits appeared when I called. Except for my parents, most of my family had forgotten I was an apprentice—I remained so ordinary. Every afternoon after school, I walked to the house of the teacher, an old wooden house surrounded by hedges of ginger. Every evening, I returned home late, to eat the dinner my mother had set aside for me alone, before starting my homework for school.

I knew only how to sit and how to listen, and I was listening for nothing. I heard only silence.

In the night, the wood of the mapes creaked, settling into the earth and there was the rainlike patter of lizards running through the leaves. Dampness clung to my skin and the seabirds called, the same repeated rasping call. I thought it impossible to sit longer.

I shifted my weight, trying to remember the direction where the road lay, but before I could stand, there was a noise. My eyes opened. The darkness was moving—a rustle, a faint creaking. Something approached beneath the trees.

I stared into the tangle of branches, but there were only shadows and I saw nothing. The rustling paused, and I could feel it searching the air. I felt the dryness in my throat. I stayed very still. Was it an animal, a man? A tupapau? It had not found me yet. It was still looking through the darkness where I sat.

The leaves shuffled; it was moving again, coming closer. I turned my eyes away and then I heard the voice of the teacher. I saw him, the way he always bent, frowning towards me. "Your breath goes in and out," he would say. Look here at the center. It is easy to be lost.

My head was heavy, as if something were pressing from above. I closed my eyes. "Don't be distracted," the teacher said. Don't look this way and that.

I took in my breath, and in the next moment, I felt a sudden quiet. All my senses had been straining, looking outside—at the trees where the unknown was moving, towards the darkness where the road might be. But then I felt the roots beneath my legs and beneath my feet. I felt the trunk along my back. I felt the absolute stillness. Above, the tree branches bent and waved in the wind, below the roots creaked within the earth, but in the center of the tree where I sat, nothing moved and it was silent.

The shadows approached and I felt a sudden weight upon my head, but they were distant and I was far removed. I was enclosed in stillness. I was lost, and in the silence, I disappeared.

The teacher was tapping my shoulder. My neck felt sore; I had fallen asleep. I opened my eyes. It was early dawn, the grove suffused with a faint grey light. The branches and leaves had turned silver and the air was like mist. I was still sitting.

The teacher looked at me gravely.

I tried to speak, but my voice was cracked and dry. "I saw nothing," I said. "I heard nothing."

He nodded his head. "Good."

"I did not sing," I said.

He smiled. "No, you were snoring."

"Will the dead sing through my voice?" I asked.

The teacher bent over me, lifting something from the top of my head. The heaviness cleared, and I saw what it was: the nut seed of the mape, without shell, perfectly smooth and unmarked. He put it in my hand. The seed was light. In my hand, it weighed hardly at all.

Contributor
Commentary

Súa Agapé

Ever since I was a little girl, I liked to draw. The place I grew up in was full of art supplies, drawings, and things that created an amazing environment.

Last year I had the opportunity to participate in the Dibuja Guatemala project for the Guatemalan Cultural Center of Spain. All the artists worked on a traveling sketchbook, drawing and capturing the Guatemalan streetlife. The sketchbooks then traveled to Spain and were exhibited in a gallery. I also had the opportunity to participate in the Glug Birmingham & Inkygoodness Poster exhibition in London and the Sketchbook Project. One of my sketchbooks traveled around the United States in a mobile library. I have also worked with Sprite by Coca-Cola Company, Ogilvy Guatemala, BBDO, Santillana Editorial, VisaNet Guatemala, and Sheik 'N Beik of New York.

Mary Archer

Sometimes writing is an act of desperation. When one is bent, writing can be the pivotal point of self-possession. My fiction piece "Death of Blossom Girl" was such an act, and a pivotal point for me.

Growing up is an ugly thing. It is both a shocking and sensitizing process as one begins to understand the horror and the gift that is life. The gift offered the main character in my story is the barest gift, and the heaviest: choice. Becoming self-determining is growing up, but no one tells you how fraught with trouble and laden with grace the process is.

My protagonist suffers many deaths, and not all of them are bad. Her world is terrible and elemental, merciless, but ultimately not unkind. It is my hope the reader will understand the forces of nature and mind in reading "Death of Blossom Girl," and how the misalignment of one with the other leads to self-deception and other misfortunes. I am thinking of arbitrary "guidance," places of port, life inescapable, and the death of a lie. I am thinking about mistakes, containment, restoration, and the means of becoming wise.

Emily A. Benton

I owe much of my love of language to the Bible and Shakespeare.

I grew up listening to Bible stories read aloud by my mother, quoted by our pastor from the pulpit, and recited by teachers in my Christian school. Starting at a young age, I read the Bible for pleasure and for spiritual understanding. In my later years, literature courses introduced me to Shakespeare, and I'd highlight Hamlet's monologues with the  same vigor as I did David's psalms. Eventually, I became a more devout follower of the language of these verses than their teachings.

In graduate school, I was working on a thesis and further wrestling with ideas of belief. I was interested in faith as it extends to phenomena—how we attach ourselves to the existence of an "other" through blurry pictures, near-death experiences, and narratives circulated as evidence through the media or folklore in support of those curiosities. I was writing poems about biblical plagues, alien abductions, and ghosts (many since exiled to a hidden archive, or so I hope.)

Simultaneously, I was studying structures of verse, and was assigned to write a sonnet—nothing out of the ordinary, but given my obsessions at the time, I didn't have to look far for a topic to fit the form.

I did not set out to write a poem with a male perspective, but like many women writers, it wasn't a stretch for me to imagine the male gaze.

I read and write out of a male tradition, and I'm well aware of the way women have been sought after by men in and outside of literature. Whereas my larger body of work draws influence from more real-world encounters, writing also allows me to step outside my own lived experience into the imaginary.

Thus, this poem embodies a number of traditions I've naturally inherited:

the pastoral, the persona, the metaphysical, the narrative, the grotesque, the phenomenal, the erotic, and of course, the love verse.

My Sasquatch may have more in common with King David than he does with me, but nonetheless, he exists on the page by my hand.

Sion Dayson

I'm always a little wary of trying to inter-pret my work. Writing rises from the subconscious. I never sit down with an idea or theme in mind. Instead, images or certain lines float to the surface and I follow them. There's obviously a very conscious aspect, too. It's almost dizzying the number of decisions we must make in a piece; I consider every word and weigh each choice carefully. But I'm also a big believer in not poking too much at the mystery. I love both the craft and the magic of storytelling.

That said, I agree with Flannery O'Connor: "I write to discover what I know"—as well as explore what I don't. So often, I'm surprised by what appears on the page. Fiction is a vehicle for fostering empathy. I frequently write from a male viewpoint, perhaps because I'm trying to better understand men.

I wrote "Metal Man" several years ago. At the time, I was newly living with a man who worked as a metalsmith. He didn't particularly resemble Mike in the story and I certainly hope I'm not as clueless as Emily, but his background in a trade I'd never before encountered firsthand provided a spark. And eventually the story's central metaphor.

A lot of my fiction has a melancholy air. This story has a much lighter tone, which I enjoyed playing in. Levity doesn't negate seriousness; I think it invites us in. I'm curious about what we think of ourselves internally—and how that picture can change when we imagine how others see us. I'm interested in how we (do or don't) connect with one another, how people situate themselves in the world. I'm forever writing about relationships. In one way or another, I'm always writing about love.

Amy Holwerda

My husband's grandfather provided the first inspiration for "Gardenia." I visited him in Coalville, England a few years before his death and toured the land where he had grown up. He could no longer remember who was prime minister, or whether he had eaten lunch that day, but as we pushed his wheelchair down dirt paths near the woods, he remembered exactly which berries were edible or poisonous, and which wildflowers could be stewed for homemade spirits. There, the natural landscape was marred by a massive, abandoned limestone quarry. A hole large enough to expose different layers of the earth. It seemed poignant, even then, that a man losing his memory should note the hollowed out earth.

As often happens in fiction, the second moment of inspiration came during random conversation at a dinner party. A man told the story of his family's decision to leave their village in India when he was an infant. The man grew up in Canada and didn't return to India until adulthood, guided by that strange pull to connect to one's long abandoned cultural heritage. He visited the village where he had been born, and to his surprise, felt no emotional connection to the place. However, on the packed train car back to Mumbai, the strong smells of travel overwhelmed him, and he found himself inexplicably weeping. Later, his mother told him how she had clutched him as an infant and wept during the same train journey forty-years earlier. We all have these sensory memories imprinted on our subconscious and know how the sudden smell of clove cigarettes or musty book pages can jolt us into sudden awareness, even when the memory cannot be immediately identified.

Fiction has the wonderful ability of connecting readers to a character's experience through the shared language of emotion. So while readers may not directly relate to the experience of, say, an underdog baseball coach seeking the pennant, or muggle starting wizardry school, we can relate to the emotions driving their decisions. I am pleased to be included in this variety of "women writing about men" because such a collection forces writers to push outside of our immediate experience and explore what we share as humans. As a young woman writing about the imagined events in an old man's life, my hope is that Saul's story will spark the reader's subconscious and resonate with their own memories of hope, love, and loss.

Lillian Howan

When I was a child, my mother told me stories about her family name. Pronounced Mu in the Hakka dialect that my parents spoke, this name means a shaman or a sorcerer. My mother had a strict sense of the truth and did not tolerate exaggeration, but I loved elaborating and embellishing the truth. My mother's stories about her Mu name fascinated me, but she was stern about not encouraging my predilection for the dramatic.

My mother was born on the island of Raiatea, where she lived with her grandparents. She told me that she had a great-uncle who was so tall that he could pluck a bird from a tree. He went to buy bread for the family early in the morning, and sometimes when he returned, he amused my mother by showing her a wild bird that he released from his hand, allowing it to fly free back into the trees. As a boy, he was trained by his teacher in the Mu village in China. The teacher taught the young boys of the village, but only one would become his true apprentice.

"What would happen to the other boys?" I asked.

My mother explained that they would learn martial arts and would grow up to farm or to sell things.

"What would happen to the apprentice?" I asked.

"He learned to put himself in a trance," said my mother. She spoke of such things subtly and indirectly. She believed that truth was complicated, multi-layered, and that words were signposts pointing in the direction of something complex and vast, beyond simple explanations.

My mother passed away in Hawai'i when I was in my twenties, and in the years after her passing, certain images would appear and reappear in my dreams: perfume bottles, birds, and their songs. Like the scent of perfume or a melody that repeats itself in one's memory, the images lingered, and I found myself dwelling on their enigma. Gradually, I began to write down words—an image, a phrase, sentence by sentence—the words seeming to grow as if the dream images were the seeds, and from these dream seeds, my stories developed, taking root in the memories of my mother's stories.

Cassandra Lane

"Day of Venus" is part of a larger work entitled Bound: Romance, Race & Redemption. This larger project began more than a decade ago as one little essay after another. I clung to the root meaning of the word essay—"to test"—as I explored connections between present day and the past.

Bound follows the main narrator's quest for marital bliss and her obsession with the 1904 lynching of her paternal great-grandfather, Burt Bridges. The lynching was an act of domestic terrorism that tore apart a marriage and family and resulted in generational repercussions. Told through the voices of Sand and her maternal grandmother, Avis, the story questions the lines between ancestral bondage and personal responsibility. This manuscript of sixty-five thousand words starts in Louisiana, transports the imagination to 1904 Mississippi, and ends in present-day California.

Pat Matsueda

Composing a poem after having breakfast with my friend Tom seemed the best way to preserve our time together. Words have sounds that, when strung together properly, produce music. And when the music strikes certain emotional notes, the result is poetry. "My Friend Looks at the Horizon" expresses the surprise of moving from ordinary words and conversation to the sometimes somber poetry of relationships.

Originally from Boston and now living in Berkeley, Tom loves the ocean and Hawai'i, regularly visiting the islands twice a year. We have known each other for over two decades, and for the last several years have shared a meal whenever he visits. In his early seventies, highly awarded as a writer, and an accomplished teacher as well, he seems to occupy a different realm of achievement. But the two of us belong to a small group of public

servants—publishers, helping people to produce books and get them into readers' hands—and this tribal connection binds us in strong ways.

Tom had been back for several days and was using a cane as a result of having had knee surgery. I had parked at Kapiʻolani Park, happy to get a parking spot and—contrary to habit—arrive early. As we sat next to the beach, under the shade of the tree, we talked about various things, and then I brought up Gerald Aikau's murder of his son and his suicide. The tragic events had happened just a few days before, and they haunted me. I'd had a strong reaction to the large picture that appeared in the Sunday paper of Aikau with his seven-year-old son, Reef. It seemed both a celebration and an indictment of fatherhood. Talking with Tom about the deaths inevitably led to talk about Eddie Aikau, the surfer who died while trying to get help for his shipmates and who made the Aikau name legendary here.

The murder of my friend Mahealani Dudoit by her husband and the husband's suicide did not occur to me then, but once I started writing "My Friend Looks at the Horizon," the association appeared—as if hauling in that net of thoughts should naturally bring her in too.

Listening to Tom that morning, it seemed that in death, as in life, he wanted to be the author, and this part of the conversation made it extraordinary. I shouldn't have been too surprised since, a few years ago, Tom published a book about his nearly dying from heart disease. And I knew death was a subject important to him, having suffered the premature passing of his father and then his mother.

The last thing we experience of friends is their leaving us for good. I was shaken to have a foreshadowing of this.

Adele Ne Jame

Although my Lebanese heritage has always influenced my writing, my more recent poems—narrative elegies that explore the effects of Lebanese diaspora—began in earnest when my daughter, Melissa, and I first traveled to Beirut in 2009 and when I made a second trip the following summer.

I had grown up hearing fragments of tragic stories my maternal grandmother, Adele, told me. One especially haunts me, the one of her mother's death which occurred during a street fight in Beirut between Christians and Muslims. Her mother, Sadie, getting word of a neighborhood street fight, ran outside to find her teenage son. Adele, a child then, ran after her. When Sadie reached the crowd, she instantly saw a knife being hurled midair at her son. She stepped in front of it to shield him. She was fatally struck and bled to death on the spot. My grandmother, aged twelve, witnessed the whole thing. Though an old woman, she never got over her mother's loss and wept every time she told the story.

My father's parents and five siblings died as a result of the war in Lebanon. They were among tens of thousands who starved to death during WWI, when the Ottoman Empire sanctioned Mount Lebanon. My father never spoke a word of it. My mother cautioned us as children not to ask questions. Because he died when I was a child, I know nothing of my father's early life.

We know such stories are not ancient history. Violence in the Middle East continues at catastrophic levels. I believe such tragedies are carried forward in the blood; these and other stories are part of my DNA. I, along with millions of Lebanese dispersed throughout the world, long to return to our homeland. Although there is a search for recovery in the writing, true recovery/return is not possible for most of us, as our other lives there were irrevocably lost long ago. But I decided upon my first visit there to learn as much about that world as I could—firsthand and through research.

With the help of distant cousins and friends, we found my father's ancestral village, Maasser El Chouf, twenty miles above Beirut in Mount Lebanon. There we heard eyewitness accounts of various wars, including the Lebanese civil war (1975–1990). The evidence of war was everywhere: pancaked buildings, broken concrete, bullet-riddled walls, posters of the dead and the missing, and countless abandoned homes. This together with all the glamour of restoration and the vitality that is the spirit of Beirut. It was heartbreaking, stunning to hear accounts of starving village children eating rotting lemons off the ground and other stories. "A Deadly Embrace" refers to the September 9, 1983, Maasser village massacre when the Druzes, who lived side by side with Christians there, slaughtered everyone they could find in a matter of five hours. I remain haunted by the abandoned homes I saw in the village, my father's included. The red clouds that hang above the mountain, above the trees called the Cedars of the Lord, seem to me to contain the atoms of those on both sides of the sectarian divide who perished there. I was moved by meetings of both Druzes and Christians who still live in the village and who continue the hard work of reconciliation.

The poems published here attempt to deal with grief on its own terms and to bear witness, in some small way, to that collective history. They are informed by collected narratives, historical accounts, and whatever poetic imaginings emerge from my immersion in the culture and landscape of that small country bordering the Mediterranean Sea.

Angela Nishimoto

The memoir, "Sex Education: A Tragicomedy of Seven Years," started with "At Sea," which I wrote when I recalled the feel of salt winds, the muted light through cloud cover on Kāneʻohe Bay, and numbing fear. I began "At Sea" at the Windward Community College Writing Retreat, headed by Lillian Cunningham. I showed this beginning to my husband, Andrew McCullough— as I do with all my writing. Then I took it to our writing group, and Pat Matsueda, Connie Pan, and Mary Archer brought me to see that it was part of a greater whole. As my memory was stirred, more began to flow. It became a tidal wave.

My poem, "Start with Mustard," was roughed out at a Hawai'i Fiction Writers meeting at the 'Āina Haina Public Library, led by Michael Little. We did a writing exercise, prompted by lines from different works by prominent African-American poets. I chose a line from a poem by the wonderful writer Maya Angelou. I was aided and abetted in refining this short piece by poets Pat Matsueda and Mary Archer. It is my first published poem.

Connie Pan

At Grand Valley State University in fall 2008, I, in my mid-twenties and laptop-less, visited the computer lab. Remembering and stealing from John Irving's creative process, I wrote the first and last sentence of a story about a teenage girl who jumped from her second-story bedroom window. A wannabe poet, I was terrified by the amount of words in a short story, and I wanted—needed—to know how and where the narrative was taking me. In the pocket of time that followed, of which I remember nothing but gleeful inspiration, I filled that empty space, writing the second sentence to the penultimate one.

Not only was "The Patron Saint of Exits" the first story I wrote for a creative writing workshop, but it was also the first story I ever wrote. Even though my professor pronounced it ready to submit to journals, I felt protective, so I hugged it fiercely—that intimate, too fresh thing—and traipsed around with it for a while. A year, my internal clock tells me. Plus, I knew nothing about literary magazines and submitting.

In the interview titled "Ancestral Voices" from The Spiral of Memory, Bill Moyers asks Joy Harjo about the recurring symbol of horses in her work. Harjo explains that while traveling from Albuquerque to Las Cruces in her "little red truck," the vision of a horse appeared to her. She stated, "I could see it at the edge of my vision, and this horse was a very old friend, someone I hadn't seen in a long time....I had tears running down from my eyes because it was so good to see this horse…I notice that for me certain forces seem to take two or three years before they come into being, and it took about that long before the poems with the horses began to emerge."

It clicked for me then. Like Harjo with her horses, I began with a surreal image of a rebellious girl falling through the night air, the fluorescent light and stars above her, determination on her face. It took several years for me to explore the magic of place and what happens when we lose those places, and people.

What began as a fourteen-page story haunted and haunted and haunted me until I continued writing. This time I didn't have the last sentence. I wrote into the unknown to find out what happened to the protagonist, Elsa, who kept eluding me, slipping out of my field of vision: out windows, into bathrooms, bedrooms, sugarcane fields, into the dark. It took, from first vision to the last drafted sentence, nearly five years to discover the answer, and now, I'm left with more questions.

While on the subject of being haunted, years ago, the grounds manager of my old apartment building told me about a murder-suicide nearby. A man, estranged from his ex, discovered where she was hiding, broke in, killed her, her friends, then himself. Terribly, this is a common headline. Margaret Atwood states, "Men are afraid that women will laugh at them. Women are afraid that men will kill them." I wrote this poem for lovers, girlfriends, and wives who have left relationships—and who were, in turn, terrorized by their exes—to challenge sexist narratives that fault women. She shouldn't have worn that. She shouldn't have dated him. She shouldn't have given him another chance. You get the idea. This damning and illogical dismissal of crime against females ignores the problem's core; the world should be raising better men, and the world should be holding men, guilty of crimes against women, accountable.

Obsessed with form and found poetry, I envisioned whole sentences and lines disfigured by a character limit, an entire page of the beginning of ignored emails from most recent to oldest. I became obsessed with creating a story this way. The form and unreliable speaker left little room for concrete context other than the title and subtitle, so I leaned on both to carry the reader through the poem. These poetic conventions gifted me three voices. First, the legal advice of a professional—because we need evidence, send his emails somewhere you don't have to see them—became the title. Second, the victim, who has taken that advice, becomes the subtitle (don't open, formatted how it would appear on her computer screen). Lastly, the stalker's many dangerous moods became the poem's body.

Shelly Rodrigue

The subject matter of my poetic craft is obsessions. Often, those obsessions are the intricacies of the characters I interact with daily. Friends and family, beware! I like to write about what strikes me most in a person, which is frequently dialect and mannerisms. In my poem, "The Fisherman's Son," I've attempted to capture polar extremes as juxtaposed in my friend's personality. The pendulum swings between crude and refined, troglodyte and gentlemanly, in a way I find oddly endearing as I celebrate the strange and humorous relationship we share. Many of my poems follow in this fashion. I take what I love about whom I love and immortalize it because I feel the world needs to know these things. There are gems in little moments, and it is these I wish to preserve in my work.

Rebecca Thomas

I didn't really start writing about Southern California until after I left. Sitting in West Virginia, I kept circling back to the neighborhoods I knew. With distance I was able to see the ways that class and race influenced the region. "Spring Training" started during a West Virginia winter with the longing for spring, the brief window of green in Southern California when wildflowers bloom before the heat comes, and

for the promise that comes with the beginning of spring training for baseball.

My character Francisco Romero reminds me of the ways that we can nav-
igate through the world: by opening ourselves up, or putting up walls. It makes
sense why Frank isolates himself. Here is a man who is grieving, who is being
pushed out of his rapidly gentrifying neighborhood, who is seeing his neighborhood's history disappear, and who is separated emotionally and geograph-
ically from his children. Frank's central question in this story speaks to the
promise of spring: will he trust in the future, in investing in the neighborhood
that he loves and grew up with, or will he continue to wall himself off?

Contributor Notes

Súa Agapé studied graphic design at the University of San Carlos in Guatemala and Digital Creativity at Digital Invaders in Mexico. She teaches illustration at the Landivar University in Guatemala, and since 2015, she has worked on her own as a designer and freelance illustrator. She is currently working on some new projects to develop her illustrations for designs on textiles. These careers complement her passion for illustration.

Mary Archer is now a University of Hawai'i at Mānoa graduate with a BA in English. In spring 2015, her essay and narrative fiction piece appeared in *Ka Hue Anahā: Journal of Academic & Research Writing*, Kapi'olani Community College's student periodical. Last year, her poetry suite, "Drafts of Robert McHenry," appeared in *Ms. Aligned: Women Writing About Men*. She is a New York native and current Hawai'i local.

Emily A. Benton is an assistant poetry editor for *storySouth* and a former poetry editor for *The Greensboro Review*. Her poems have been published in *Hawai'i Review, Hawai'i Pacific Review, Hayden's Ferry Review, Barn Owl Review, Southern Poetry Review, Harpur Palate,* and other journals. She holds a BA in communication from Queens University of Charlotte and an MFA in creative writing from the University of North Carolina at Greensboro. Originally from Tennessee, she has lived in Hawai'i since 2012.

Sion Dayson is an American/French dual citizen splitting her time between the United States and Europe. Her work has appeared in *The Writer, The Rumpus, Electric Literature, Hunger Mountain, Utne Reader, The Wall Street Journal, Courrier International, Numero Cinq,* and several anthologies, including *James Baldwin: Challenging Authors, Strangers in Paris,* and *Seek It: Writers and Artists Do Sleep*. She holds an MFA in fiction from Vermont College of Fine Arts and has blogged about the quirkier side of the City of Light for several years at *paris (im)perfect*. Sion has been awarded residencies and grants from the Kerouac House, the Money for Women/Barbara Deming Memorial Fund, and the Stone Court Writer-in-Residence program. Her first novel manuscript, which also features a male protagonist, placed on the short list for finalists in the William Faulkner–William Wisdom Creative Writing Competition.

Amy Holwerda lives and writes in Chicago, Illinois. Her work has been noted in *Best American Essays* (2013), and has appeared in *The Collagist, Hobart, Flash International, The Sycamore Review, Quick Fiction,* and elsewhere.

Lillian Howan spent her early childhood in Tahiti and later graduated from the University of California, Berkeley, School of Law. Her writings have been published in *Asian American Literary Review, Café Irreal, Calyx, New England Review,* and the anthology *Under Western Eyes.* She is the editor of *Rosebud and Other Stories,* a collection by legendary playwright Wakako Yamauchi, and the author of the novel *The Charm Buyers.*

Gerda Govine Ituarte's third poetry collection, *Future Awakes in Mouth of NOW,* was published by Editions du Cygne (Swan World, Paris, 2016). Her second poetry book, *Alterations | Thread Light Through Eye of Storm,* was published in 2015 in Mexico City and was a finalist in *Red City Review*'s poetry contest. Her first book, *Oh, Where is My Candle Hat?,* was published in English and Spanish in Tijuana, Mexico, in 2012. In 2016, *Spectrum Magazine* selected her as one of the top ten poets in Los Angeles. As CEO of G. Govine Consulting, she conducts diversity and inclusion climate studies, provides training and workshops, and serves as an expert witness, litigation consultant, investigator, and mediator in the areas of gender, race, and age discrimination. Born in St. Thomas, Virgin Islands, she also serves as a member of the Los Angeles County Women's Commission and of the City of Pasadena Sister City Advisory Group.

Jill McCabe Johnson is the author of the poetry books *Revolutions We'd Hoped We'd Outgrown* (Finishing Line, 2017) and *Diary of the One Swelling Sea* (MoonPath, 2013), winner of a Nautilus Book Award, plus the nonfiction chapbook *Borderlines* (Sweet Publications, 2016). She is series editor for the University of Nebraska Gender Programs anthologies, including *Becoming: What Makes a Woman* and *Being: What Makes a Man.* Honors include an Artist Trust grant, an Academy of American Poets Award, the Mari Sandoz Prairie Schooner Prize in Fiction, Scissortale Review's Editor's Prize in Poetry, plus the Deborah Tall Memorial Fellowship from Pacific Lutheran University, where she completed her MFA in Creative Writing, and the Louise Van Sickle Fellowship in Poetry from the University of Nebraska, where she received her PhD in English with an Interdisciplinary Specialization in Nineteenth Century Studies. Johnson teaches creative writing and English at Skagit Valley College and is the founding director of Artsmith, a non-profit to support the arts.

Kristiana Kahakauwila is the author of *This is Paradise: Stories* (Hogarth, 2013), a Barnes & Noble Discover selection. She is an associate professor of creative writing at Western Washington University and was a 2015–2016 fellow at Harvard University's Radcliffe Institute of Advanced Study. Her most recent work has appeared in *Kartika Review, Mistake House,* and RED INK: *An International Journal of Indigenous Literature, Arts, & Humanities.* Currently, she is working on a multigenerational historical novel set on the island of Maui.

Cassandra Lane is a former newspaper reporter and high school literature and journalism teacher who has published essays, columns, and articles in many newspapers, magazines and anthologies. She is an alum of Voices of Our Nation Arts (VONA) Foundation and A Room of Her Own (AROHO), and received an MFA in creative writing from Antioch University. A Louisiana native, she lives with her family in Los Angeles and is the managing editor of *L.A. Parent* magazine.

Pat Matsueda is the managing editor of *Mānoa: A Pacific Journal of International Writing* and the author of *Stray* (2006) and *Bedeviled* (2016, 2017). She coedited the 2016 edition of *Ms. Aligned* with Sheyene Foster Heller and has a small business, Peak Services, which provides editorial and publishing services to individuals and organizations.

Adele Ne Jame teaches poetry at Hawai'i Pacific University. She served for a year as the Poet-in-Residence at the University of Wisconsin-Madison and has published four books of poems. Her honors include a Pablo Neruda prize for poetry, a National Endowment for the Arts fellowship in poetry, an Elliot Cades Award for Literature, and the 2016 Robinson Jeffers Tor House Foundation Poetry Award. Her poems were exhibited as broadsides in the United Arab Emirates International Biennial 2009. Of the poems in her most recent collection, *The South Wind,* one reviewer noted that "her continuous awareness of the overlapping realms of life and death are what give her work its emotional heft."

Angela Nishimoto was raised on the windward side of O'ahu, teaches on the leeward side, and lives in Honolulu with her husband. She earned her master-of-science degree in botanical science at the University of Hawai'i at Mānoa. She has published fiction in *Hawai'i Pacific Review, Chaminade Literary Review, Kaimana, Hawai'i Review, Bamboo Ridge, Writing Raw, Ms. Aligned,* and elsewhere. "Sex Education: A Tragicomedy of Seven Years" is from a longer nonfiction work.

Connie Pan, originally from Maui, earned an MFA in fiction from West Virginia University and a BA in creative writing from Grand Valley State University. Her writing has appeared or is forthcoming in *The Fiddlehead, Carve, PRISM international, Rosebud, Bamboo Ridge,* and elsewhere. An excerpt from her novel-in-progress was nominated for a Pushcart Prize. A freelance writer and editor, she lives in California.

Shelly Rodrigue is a poet from New Orleans, Louisiana. She obtained a BA in English from the University of Holy Cross and is currently pursuing an MFA at the University of New Orleans. Her poems have appeared in *Guide to Kulchur Creative Journal, The Borfski Press, Fourth & Sycamore,* and *Ellipsis.* She is the 2017 recipient of the Andrea Saunders Gereighty Academy of American Poets Poetry Award. When she is not writing, she enjoys playing guitar as well as kayaking. She is the former rhythm guitarist of New Orleans funk-rock band Pulp Deception. Currently, she teaches English as a second language to children in China through an online platform. She also works as an ethnographer for UNO Chart.

Rebecca Thomas's fiction and nonfiction have appeared in *Prairie Schooner, Hunger Mountain, The Massachusetts Review, Fifth Wednesday,* and other journals. In 2015, she received a Pushcart Prize nomination for fiction. She received her MFA in creative writing from West Virginia University. She received undergraduate degrees in creative writing and screenwriting from Chapman University. Originally from Orange County, California, she now teaches writing in Morgantown, West Virginia.

Permissions and Acknowledgements

"Sasquatch in Love" by Emily Benton was first published in *Waccamaw: A Journal of Contemporary Literature.*

"Metal Man" by Sion Dayson was first published in *Ms. Aligned: Women Writing About Men* (Aligned Press, 2016).

"Gardenia" by Amy Holwerda was first published in *Room* in 2014.

"I Love When" by Gerda Govine Ituarte was first published in *Oh, Where is My Candle Hat?* (Asterisco, Tijuana, 2012).

"Veteran" by Gerda Govine Ituarte was first published in *Frontera Esquina Magazine* in 2013. "Veteran" was also published in *Future Awakes in Mouth of NOW* (Editions du Cygne/Swan World, Paris, 2016).

"Grief, A Revolving Landscape" by Adele Ne Jame was also published in *Rusted Radishes: Beirut Literary & Art Journal.*

"Because We Need Evidence, Send His Emails Somewhere You Don't Have to See Them" by Connie Pan was first published in *Ms. Aligned: Women Writing About Men* (Aligned Press, 2016).

"The Patron Saint of Exits" by Connie Pan was first published in *Rosebud* in 2010.

"Spring Training" by Rebecca Thomas was first published in *The Massachusetts Review* in fall 2015.

 A thousand thanks to all the people who supported the *Ms. Aligned* project and helped to make this book possible: Suzanne

Casart, Frances Enos, Kazuyo Karan, Chelsea Kerrington, Alan Mawyer, Ron Schoenmehl, Shane Stricker, Shari Tamashiro, Laurie Van Tuinen, Jim Wageman, Sarah Yasutake, Phyllis Young, and Dr. Monique Yuen. Special thanks to the following: the University of Hawai'i at Mānoa's SEED IDEAS program, which supported this project with a grant, and Michael Schmicker and Richard Tillotson, who provided promotion and marketing help.

Ms. Aligned
Women Writing About Men

Edited by Pat Matsueda and Sheyene Foster Heller

"The writings in *Ms. Aligned* are, in the original sense of the word, astonishing—yes, they surprise us, but they also stun, bewilder, and dismay. Whatever the best expectations for such a collection may be, this one lives up to them. And more important, it exceeds them." *Hayan Charara*

"The female perspectives presented here—male creations/female creators—dissect, prod, query, challenge, validate, negotiate, and, ultimately, emancipate the gender boundaries that we otherwise take for granted. The effect is a wonderful loosening of the physical world, of our selves." *Samrat Upadhyay*

"For too long, males have gazed on the female form and explained it. Here, we find female writers identifying what is malehood / what is masculine / what is the essence of being for those of the opposite sex. They gaze on the male form and explain it. We need more of this balancing in literature." *Shane Stricker*

Aligned Press, 2016

$4.99 • ISBN 978-1-3299707-7-9 • 133 pages

msaligned.com

The South Wind
by Adele Ne Jame

"Has so much richness in spirit and
depth of soul in it. Such gifts as this
poetry offers—a lyric voice that
weaves those elements together with
an historical consciousness, from the
personal to the political, across a wide
canvas—are both
unusual and admirable."
Alan Botsford
editor of *Poetry Kanto*

"Distilling the bittersweet, capturing
what it means to be creatures
in love with a fleeting world of
wonders—this is the specialty of
poets. Adele Ne Jame's poems are
lovely examples of the art."
Teresa Scollon
ForeWord Book Reviews

2011 · 32 PAGES
ISBN 978-0-9833919-0-6

Bedeviled
by Pat Matsueda

"A beautiful metaphor, surprising,
riveting, and honest. Within its
pages, Internet porn and the
floating world seem made for
each other, and are grounded in
the human heart. The prose is
spare and searching; the overall
effect is luminous."
Robert Shapard
coeditor of *Flash Fiction International*

"Told with charity, clarity, and
insight, this story of an unassuming
Everyman who has tried—and
failed—to 'lead his life by the book'
is a compelling and touching read.
I loved *Bedeviled* and hope it
finds a wide readership."
Molly Giles
author of *All the Wrong Places*

2017 · 128 PAGES
ISBN 978-0-9799504-0-7

PUBLICATIONS FROM

MĀNOA BOOKS
HONOLULU
manoafoundation.org

EL LEÓN LITERARY ARTS
BERKELEY
elleonliteraryarts.org